cooking with herbs & spices

THE AUSTRALIAN
Women's Weekly

contents

Fresh herbs and jars of rich spices are every cook's secret treasure trove to create great-tasting, flavour-filled food. For the freshest herbs, get a pot on your window-sill or cultivate some of the supermarket pots – then just pick off what you want when you need it. To add rich aromatic tastes to your cooking, use spices such as ginger and sweet paprika to build up the layers for perfectly satisfying food.

Food Director

Pamela Clark

glazed-chicken tortilla with sprout & herb salad

¼ cup (80g) cranberry sauce
1 tablespoon wholegrain mustard
1 tablespoon lemon juice
5cm piece fresh ginger (25g), grated
1 clove garlic, crushed
500g chicken breast fillets
1 small red onion (100g), sliced thinly
60g mangetout sprouts
¼ cup shredded fresh coriander
¼ cup shredded fresh mint
1 tablespoon white wine vinegar
4 large flour tortillas

1 Heat combined sauce, mustard, juice, ginger and garlic in small saucepan, stirring, until glaze comes to a boil.
2 Cook chicken, in batches, in heated lightly oiled large frying pan, brushing frequently with glaze, until cooked through. Cover chicken; stand 5 minutes before slicing thickly.
3 Meanwhile, place onion, sprouts, herbs and vinegar in medium bowl; toss salad gently to combine. Heat tortillas according to manufacturer's instructions.
4 Divide chicken and salad among centres of the tortillas; roll tortillas around filling to form cones.

preparation time 15 minutes
cooking time 20 minutes
serves 4
per serving 5.6g fat; 1296kJ (310 cal)

Whether it's Sunday morning brunch, a tasty afternoon treat or a quick filler before dashing off for an evening out, these snacks are not only delicious but imaginative as well!

bruschetta...

prawn & lime mayonnaise

2 tablespoons low-fat mayonnaise
2 teaspoons finely chopped fresh dill
1 tablespoon lime juice
2 slices ciabatta
10g baby rocket leaves
8 cooked small prawns

1 Make lime mayonnaise by combining the mayonnaise, dill and lime juice.
2 Toast the ciabatta slices; divide the rocket leaves, prawns and mayonnaise mixture between both slices.

preparation time 10 minutes
cooking time 2 minutes
serves 1
per serving 7.6g fat; 1158kJ (277 cal)

smoked chicken & mango chutney

2 slices ciabatta
1 teaspoon low-fat mayonnaise
1 teaspoon finely chopped fresh chives
100g smoked chicken, thinly sliced
10g mixed herb salad leaves
1 tablespoon mango chutney

1 Toast the ciabatta slices.
2 Combine the mayonnaise with the chives and spread over both slices, then divide the smoked chicken, herb salad and mango chutney between the slices.

preparation time 5 minutes
cooking time 2 minutes
serves 1
per serving 9.6g fat; 1605kJ (384 cal)

herby tuna salad bruschetta

95g can drained tuna in brine
1 tablespoon low-fat mayonnaise
½ small red onion, finely chopped
1 tablespoon coarsely chopped fresh
    flat-leaf parsley
1 tablespoon coarsely chopped fresh
    chives
2 slices ciabatta

1 Combine the tuna, mayonnaise, onion,
flat-leaf parsley and chives in a small bowl.
2 Toast the ciabatta slices; divide tuna salad
between the slices.

preparation time 5 minutes
cooking time 2 minutes
serves 1
per serving 6.5g fat; 1304kJ (312 cal)

ham, tomato & avocado

1 medium plum tomato
2 teaspoons brown sugar
2 slices ciabatta
¼ small avocado, sliced
50g wafer-thin ham
cayenne pepper

1 Preheat oven to moderate.
2 Cut tomato in half. Place tomato halves,
cut-side up, on an oven tray, sprinkle with
sugar. Cook, uncovered, in moderate oven for
20 minutes.
3 Toast the ciabatta slices; divide the avocado,
ham and tomato halves between slices.
4 Sprinkle with cayenne pepper to taste.

preparation time 5 minutes
cooking time 25 minutes
serves 1
per serving 11.6g fat; 1367kJ (327 cal)

strawberry, banana & cinnamon ricotta bruschetta

½ loaf ciabatta (220g)
200g low-fat ricotta
2 tablespoons honey
1 teaspoon finely grated orange rind
¼ teaspoon ground cinnamon
125g strawberries, sliced thickly
1 small banana (130g), sliced thinly
2 tablespoons brown sugar

1　Preheat grill.
2　Trim end from bread; cut into eight slices.
3　Beat ricotta, honey, rind and cinnamon in small bowl with electric mixer until smooth.
4　Combine strawberries, banana and sugar in small frying pan; stir gently over low heat until sugar dissolves.
5　Meanwhile, toast bread both sides. Spread with ricotta mixture, divide among plates; top with strawberry mixture.

preparation time 15 minutes
cooking time 10 minutes
serves 4
per serving 5.8g fat; 1208kJ (289 cal)

sautéed mushroom bruschetta

30g butter
200g chestnut mushrooms, sliced thickly
100g fresh shiitake mushrooms, sliced thickly
200g button mushrooms, halved
100g oyster mushrooms, halved
1 clove garlic, crushed
¼ cup (60ml) beef stock
½ loaf ciabatta (220g)
¼ cup chopped fresh flat-leaf parsley
¼ cup chopped fresh chives

preparation time 10 minutes
cooking time 20 minutes
serves 4
per serving 8.1g fat; 966kJ (231 cal)

1 Preheat grill.
2 Melt butter in large frying pan; cook mushrooms and garlic, stirring, about 5 minutes. Add stock; bring to a boil. Reduce heat; simmer, uncovered, about 10 minutes or until mushrooms are cooked as desired.
3 Meanwhile, trim end from bread; cut into eight slices. Toast bread both sides; divide among serving plates. Stir herbs into mushrooms; serve on toast.

smoked salmon & cream cheese bruschetta

⅓ cup (80g) light cream cheese
1 shallot (25g), chopped finely
2 teaspoons lemon juice
½ teaspoon dijon mustard
1 tablespoon chopped fresh dill
1 tablespoon drained capers, rinsed, chopped coarsely
1 loaf sourdough bread (675g)
30g baby rocket leaves
200g sliced smoked salmon

preparation time 15 minutes
cooking time 5 minutes
serves 4
per serving 10.1g fat; 2153kJ (515 cal)

1 Preheat grill.
2 Combine cream cheese, shallot, juice, mustard, dill and capers in small bowl.
3 Trim ends from bread, cut into eight slices. Toast bread both sides. Spread cheese mixture over toast; divide among plates. Top with rocket and salmon.

spicy parmesan seed twists

1 sheet ready-rolled puff pastry, halved
1 egg yolk
1 tablespoon poppy seeds
2 teaspoons mustard seeds
1 teaspoon sweet paprika
½ teaspoon salt
2 tablespoons finely grated parmesan

1 Preheat oven to moderately hot. Grease and line two baking trays.
2 Brush pastry halves with egg on one side; sprinkle with combined seeds, paprika and salt. Turn over one of the halves so unseeded side faces up; brush with egg, sprinkle with parmesan. Sandwich the two halves with parmesan side in the centre and two seeded sides facing out; press down firmly.
3 Cut pastry widthways into 24 strips; twist each strip, pinching ends to seal. Place twists on prepared trays; bake, uncovered, in moderately hot oven about 15 minutes or until browned lightly.

preparation time 15 minutes
cooking time 15 minutes
makes 24
per twist 2.2g fat; 138kJ (33 cal)

polenta & chilli cheese muffins

2 cups (300g) self-raising flour
2 teaspoons caster sugar
½ cup (85g) polenta
250g low-fat cottage cheese
⅓ cup (25g) coarsely grated parmesan
½ teaspoon dried chilli flakes
4 spring onions, chopped finely
1 egg
1 cup (250ml) skimmed milk
2 tablespoons vegetable oil

1 Preheat oven to moderately hot. Lightly grease 12-hole (⅓-cup/80ml) muffin tray.
2 Combine flour, sugar and ⅓ cup of the polenta in medium bowl with cottage cheese, parmesan, chilli and onion. Stir in combined egg, milk and oil.
3 Divide mixture among prepared holes of muffin tray; sprinkle with remaining polenta.
4 Bake, uncovered, in moderately hot oven about 20 minutes. Stand muffins in tray 5 minutes; turn onto wire rack to cool.

preparation time 20 minutes
cooking time 20 minutes
makes 12
per muffin 5.2g fat; 796kJ (184 cal)

tom yum goong

Tom yums are the most popular soups in Thailand. Translated loosely as broth or stock (tom) and combined spicy sour (yum), this soup is far more than the name would indicate. Sour and tangy, without the sweetness of coconut, tom yum goong's unique taste comes from the combination of spicy ingredients, like chilli and curry paste, with sour ones like lime juice and tamarind.

900g uncooked large king prawns
1 tablespoon groundnut oil
1.5 litres (6 cups) water
2 tablespoons red curry paste
1 tablespoon tamarind concentrate
10cm stick fresh lemongrass (20g), chopped finely
1 teaspoon ground turmeric
2 fresh small red thai chillies, chopped coarsely
1cm piece fresh ginger (5g), grated
6 fresh kaffir lime leaves, shredded finely
1 teaspoon grated palm sugar
100g fresh shiitake mushrooms, halved
2 tablespoons fish sauce
2 tablespoons lime juice
¼ cup loosely packed vietnamese mint leaves
¼ cup loosely packed fresh coriander leaves

1 Shell and devein prawns, leaving tails intact; reserve heads and shells.
2 Heat oil in large saucepan; cook prawn shells and heads, stirring, about 5 minutes or until a deep orange in colour.
3 Add 1 cup of the water and curry paste to pan; bring to a boil, stirring. Add remaining water; return to a boil. Reduce heat; simmer, uncovered, 20 minutes. Strain broth through muslin-lined sieve or colander into large heatproof bowl; discard solids.
4 Return broth to same cleaned pan. Add tamarind, lemongrass, turmeric, chilli, ginger, lime leaf and sugar; bring to a boil. Boil, stirring, 2 minutes. Add mushrooms, reduce heat; cook, stirring, 3 minutes. Add prawns; simmer, uncovered, about 5 minutes or until prawns are cooked as desired. Remove from heat; stir in sauce and juice.
5 Serve bowls of soup sprinkled with mint and coriander.

preparation time 20 minutes
cooking time 40 minutes
serves 4
per serving 9g fat; 849kJ (203 cal)

Soup, the world's best known 'bowl food', is a meal in a single take. From a clear and delicate Asian broth to a hearty peasant stew, soups cover all the right bases – aroma, flavour, texture and substance.

spiced coriander, lentil & barley soup

1 tablespoon coriander seeds
1 tablespoon cumin seeds
1 tablespoon ghee
6 cloves garlic, crushed
2 fresh small red thai chillies, chopped finely
1¼ cups (250g) soup mix
1 litre (4 cups) chicken stock
3½ cups (875ml) water
1 cup coarsely chopped fresh coriander
⅓ cup (95g) greek-style plain yogurt
1 tablespoon mango chutney

1 Dry-fry seeds in large saucepan, stirring, until fragrant. Using pestle and mortar, crush seeds.
2 Melt ghee in same pan; cook crushed seeds, garlic and chilli, stirring, 5 minutes.
3 Add soup mix, stock and the water; bring to a boil. Reduce heat; simmer, covered, stirring occasionally, 1 hour. Cool 15 minutes.
4 Blend or process half the soup, in batches, until smooth. Return pureed soup to pan with unprocessed soup; stir over medium heat until hot. Remove from heat; stir in coriander.
5 Serve bowls of soup topped with yogurt and a little mango chutney.

preparation time 10 minutes (plus cooling time)
cooking time 1 hour 20 minutes
serves 4
per serving 7.9g fat; 1350kJ (323 cal)
tip Soup mix is a packaged blend of various dried pulses and grains, among them, lentils, split peas and barley. It is available from supermarkets.

harira

After sundown during Ramadan, many of the Muslims in Morocco break the day's fast by starting their meal with this hearty, nourishing soup. Recipes vary from family to family, but chickpeas and lamb always feature.

1 cup (200g) dried chickpeas
20g butter
2 medium brown onions (300g), chopped finely
2 trimmed celery stalks (200g), chopped finely
2 cloves garlic, crushed
4cm piece fresh ginger (20g), grated
1 teaspoon ground cinnamon
½ teaspoon ground black pepper
pinch saffron threads
500g diced lamb
3 large tomatoes (660g), deseeded, chopped coarsely
2 litres (8 cups) hot water
½ cup (100g) brown lentils
2 tablespoons plain flour
½ cup (100g) white long-grain rice
½ cup firmly packed fresh coriander leaves
2 tablespoons lemon juice

---

preparation time 25 minutes (plus standing time)
cooking time 2 hours 15 minutes
serves 8
per serving 8.6g fat; 1095kJ (262 cal)

---

1 Place chickpeas in medium bowl, cover with water, stand overnight; drain. Rinse under cold water; drain.
2 Melt butter in large saucepan; cook onion, celery and garlic, stirring, until onion softens. Add ginger, cinnamon, pepper and saffron; cook, stirring, until fragrant. Add lamb; cook, stirring, about 5 minutes or until lamb is browned. Add chickpeas and tomato; cook, stirring, about 5 minutes or until tomato softens.
3 Stir the water into soup mixture; bring to a boil. Reduce heat; simmer, covered, 45 minutes. Add lentils; simmer, covered, 1 hour.
4 Blend flour with ½ cup of slightly cooled broth in a small bowl; return to pan with rice. Cook, stirring, until soup comes to a boil and thickens slightly. Remove from heat; stir in coriander and juice.

chicken, chorizo & okra gumbo

3 litres (12 cups) water
1.5kg whole chicken
2 medium carrots (240g), chopped
  coarsely
2 trimmed celery stalks (200g),
  chopped coarsely
1 medium brown onion (150g),
  chopped coarsely
12 black peppercorns
1 bay leaf
60g butter
1 small brown onion (80g), chopped
  finely, extra
2 cloves garlic, crushed
1 medium red pepper (200g), chopped
  finely
2 teaspoons dried oregano
1 teaspoon sweet paprika
¼ teaspoon cayenne pepper
¼ teaspoon ground cloves
¼ cup (35g) plain flour
¼ cup (70g) tomato paste
400g can crushed tomatoes
100g fresh okra, halved diagonally
1 cup (200g) short-grained rice
1 chorizo sausage (170g), sliced thinly

1 Place the water in large saucepan with chicken, carrot, celery, onion, peppercorns and bay leaf; bring to a boil. Reduce heat; simmer, covered, 1½ hours.
2 Remove chicken from pan. Strain broth through muslin-lined sieve or colander into large heatproof bowl; discard solids. When chicken is cool enough to handle, remove and discard skin and bones; shred meat coarsely.
3 Melt butter in large saucepan; cook extra onion and garlic, stirring, until onion softens. Add pepper, herbs and spices; cook, stirring, until mixture is fragrant. Add flour and paste; cook, stirring, 1 minute. Gradually stir in reserved broth and undrained tomatoes; bring to a boil, stirring. Stir in okra and rice, reduce heat; simmer, uncovered, about 15 minutes, stirring occasionally, or until rice is tender.
4 Meanwhile, heat large oiled frying pan; cook sausage until browned; drain. Add sausage with chicken to gumbo; stir over medium heat until hot.

preparation time 30 minutes
cooking time 2 hours 45 minutes
serves 8
per serving 26.8g fat; 2011kJ (481 cal)
tip If you want to cook this gumbo a day ahead, the flavours will meld and deepen, making the soup even more delicious. Follow the recipe through to the end of step 2 then cool the soup, cover and refrigerate it overnight.

hungarian goulash

2 tablespoons olive oil
40g butter
900g boneless veal shoulder, diced into
    2cm pieces
2 medium brown onions (300g),
    chopped finely
1 tablespoon tomato paste
1 tablespoon plain flour
1 tablespoon sweet paprika
2 teaspoons caraway seeds
½ teaspoon cayenne pepper
2 cloves garlic, crushed
2 cups (500ml) water
1.5 litres (6 cups) beef stock
400g can crushed tomatoes
1 large red pepper (350g), chopped
    coarsely
1 medium potato (200g), chopped
    coarsely

spätzle
1 cup (150g) plain flour
2 eggs, beaten lightly
¼ cup (60ml) water
½ teaspoon cracked black pepper

1 Heat half the oil and half the butter in large saucepan; cook veal, in batches, until browned all over.
2 Heat remaining oil and remaining butter in same pan; cook onion, stirring, about 5 minutes or until onion is slightly caramelised.
3 Add paste, flour, paprika, seeds, cayenne and garlic; cook, stirring, 2 minutes. Return veal to pan with the water, stock and undrained tomatoes; bring to a boil. Reduce heat; simmer, uncovered, 1½ hours. Add pepper and potato; simmer, uncovered, about 10 minutes or until potato is tender.
4 Meanwhile, make spätzle.
5 Serve bowls of soup topped with spätzle.

spätzle Place flour in small bowl, make well in centre. Gradually add combined egg and the water, stirring, until batter is smooth; stir in pepper. Pour batter into metal colander set over large saucepan of boiling water; using a wooden spoon, push batter through holes of colander. Bring water back to a boil; boil, uncovered, about 2 minutes or until spätzle float to the surface. Use a slotted spoon to remove spätzle; drain before adding to goulash soup.

preparation time 25 minutes
cooking time 2 hours
serves 4
per serving 27.3g fat; 3022kJ (723 cal)
tip Spätzle, served throughout Austria, Germany, Switzerland and the French region of Alsace, are tiny noodle-like dumplings made by pushing a batter through the holes of a colander or strainer into a pan of boiling water or stock. The cooked spätzle are generally tossed in a frying pan with melted butter before being served.

fast soups...

chicken & sweetcorn

25g canned creamed sweetcorn
½ cup shredded cooked chicken
1 tablespoon soy sauce
½ teaspoon sambal oelek
375ml carton salt-reduced chicken stock
2 tablespoons coarsely chopped fresh
   flat-leaf parsley

1 Combine the sweetcorn, chicken, soy
sauce and sambal oelek in a medium
microwave-safe bowl.
2 Stir in the chicken stock.
3 Cook, uncovered, on HIGH (100%) in
microwave oven about 2 minutes or until hot.
4 Sprinkle with the flat-leaf parsley before
serving.

preparation time 5 minutes
cooking time 2 minutes
serves 1
per serving 7.4g fat; 1024kJ (245 cal)

thai chicken noodle

½ cup cooked chicken, thinly sliced
1 teaspoon red curry paste
175g packet singapore noodles
375ml carton salt-reduced chicken stock
1 tablespoon coarsely chopped fresh
   coriander
½ spring onion, thinly sliced

1 Combine the chicken and curry paste in a
medium microwave-safe bowl.
2 Rinse noodles under hot water. Add the
noodles to the chicken mixture with the stock.
3 Cook, uncovered, on HIGH (100%) in
microwave oven about 2 minutes or until hot.
4 Sprinkle with coriander and spring onion
before serving.

preparation time 5 minutes
cooking time 2 minutes
serves 1
per serving 10.4g fat; 2617kJ (626 cal)

french onion

1 medium brown onion, thinly sliced
2 teaspoons olive oil
2 teaspoons brown sugar
375ml carton salt-reduced beef stock
1 bay leaf
1 teaspoon coarsely chopped fresh chives.

1 Cook the onion in the olive oil in small frying pan, stirring, until onion softens.
2 Add the sugar, then continue to cook, stirring occasionally, about 10 minutes or until onion caramelises.
3 Place onion mixture in medium microwave-safe bowl with the stock and bay leaf. Cook, uncovered, on HIGH (100%) in microwave oven about 2 minutes or until hot; remove bay leaf.
4 Sprinkle with chives before serving.

preparation time 5 minutes
cooking time 15 minutes
serves 1
per serving 10g fat; 702kJ (168 cal)

risoni & spring vegetable

¼ cup risoni (or any small soup pasta)
2 green beans, thinly sliced
1 small carrot, thinly sliced
375ml carton salt-reduced chicken or
    vegetable stock
1 tablespoon shredded fresh basil

1 Cook the risoni in small saucepan of boiling water, uncovered, until almost tender.
2 Add the green beans and carrot; then continue to cook, uncovered, for 1 minute. Drain.
3 Place risoni mixture in medium microwave-safe bowl; stir in the stock. Cook, uncovered, on HIGH (100%) in microwave oven about 2 minutes or until hot.
4 Sprinkle with basil before serving.

preparation time 5 minutes
cooking time 10 minutes
serves 1
per serving 2.2g fat; 1016kJ (243 cal)

minestrone

2 ham hocks (1kg)
1 medium brown onion (150g),
    quartered
1 trimmed celery stalk (100g), chopped
    coarsely
1 teaspoon black peppercorns
1 bay leaf
4 litres (16 cups) water
1 tablespoon olive oil
2 trimmed celery stalks (200g),
    chopped finely
1 large carrot (180g), chopped finely
3 cloves garlic, crushed
¼ cup (70g) tomato paste
2 large tomatoes (440g), chopped
    finely
1 small leek (200g), sliced thinly
1 cup (100g) small pasta shells
420g can cannellini beans, rinsed,
    drained
½ cup coarsely chopped fresh flat-leaf
    parsley
½ cup coarsely chopped fresh basil
½ cup (40g) shaved parmesan

1 Preheat oven to 220°C/200°C fan-assisted.
2 Roast hocks and onion in baking dish, uncovered,
30 minutes. Combine with coarsely chopped celery,
peppercorns, bay leaf and the water in large pan;
bring to a boil. Simmer, uncovered, 2 hours.
3 Remove hocks from soup. Strain broth through
muslin-lined sieve or colander into large heatproof
bowl; discard solids. Allow broth to cool, cover;
refrigerate until cold. When cool, remove ham from
bones; shred coarsely. Discard bones.
4 Meanwhile, heat oil in large saucepan; cook
finely chopped celery and carrot, stirring, 2 minutes.
Add ham, garlic, paste and tomato; cook, stirring,
2 minutes.
5 Discard fat from surface of broth. Place broth in
measuring jug; add enough water to make 2 litres.
Add broth to pan; bring to a boil. Simmer, covered,
20 minutes.
6 Add leek, pasta and beans; bring to a boil. Simmer,
uncovered, until pasta is just tender. Remove from
heat; stir in herbs. Serve soup sprinkled with cheese.

preparation time 40 minutes (plus refrigeration time)
cooking time 3 hours 35 minutes
serves 6
per serving 7.2g fat; 865kJ (207 cal)
tip You can make the broth either the day before or
in the morning of the day you want to finish preparing
the minestrone so that it chills long enough for the
fat to solidify on top; skim it away before reheating
the broth.

green pea soup with mint pistou

1 tablespoon olive oil
1 small leek (200g), sliced thinly
1 clove garlic, crushed
2 large potatoes (600g), chopped
   coarsely
3 cups (360g) frozen peas
3 cups (750ml) water
2 cups (500ml) vegetable stock

mint pistou
2 cups loosely packed fresh mint leaves
¼ cup (20g) finely grated parmesan
1 tablespoon lemon juice
1 clove garlic, quartered
¼ cup (60ml) olive oil

1 Heat oil in large saucepan; cook leek and garlic, stirring, until leek softens. Add potato, peas, the water and stock; bring to a boil. Reduce heat; simmer, covered, about 10 minutes or until potato is tender. Cool 15 minutes.
2 Meanwhile, make mint pistou.
3 Blend or process soup, in batches, until smooth. Return soup to same cleaned pan; stir over medium heat until hot.
4 Serve bowls of soup topped with pistou.

mint pistou Blend or process ingredients until smooth.

preparation time 10 minutes (plus cooling time)
cooking time 20 minutes
serves 4
per serving 20.9g fat; 1634kJ (391 cal)

curried cauliflower soup

1 tablespoon olive oil

1 medium brown onion (150g), chopped finely

2 cloves garlic, crushed

½ cup (150g) mild curry paste

2 litres (8 cups) water

1 small cauliflower (1kg), trimmed, chopped coarsely

2 medium potatoes (400g), chopped coarsely

1 tablespoon tomato paste

1 cup (250ml) buttermilk

½ cup loosely packed fresh coriander leaves

1 Heat oil in large saucepan; cook onion and garlic, stirring, until onion softens. Add curry paste; cook, stirring, 5 minutes.

2 Add the water, cauliflower, potato and paste; bring to a boil. Reduce heat; simmer, uncovered, about 15 minutes or until vegetables are tender. Cool 15 minutes.

3 Blend or process soup, in batches, until smooth. Return soup to same cleaned pan, add buttermilk; stir over low heat until hot.

4 Serve bowls of soup sprinkled with coriander and, if desired, accompanied with warmed naan bread.

preparation time 20 minutes (plus cooling time)
cooking time 25 minutes
serves 6
per serving 12.1g fat; 936kJ (224 cal)

25

herb-stuffed chicken with tomato salad

¼ cup finely chopped fresh basil
1 tablespoon finely chopped fresh oregano
2 teaspoons fresh lemon thyme
2 cloves garlic, crushed
1 tablespoon finely grated lemon rind
4 single chicken breast fillets (680g)
4 slices prosciutto (60g)
250g cherry tomatoes
250g teardrop tomatoes
150g baby spinach leaves
½ cup coarsely chopped fresh basil
2 tablespoons red wine vinegar
2 teaspoons olive oil

1 Preheat oven to moderate.
2 Combine finely chopped basil, oregano, thyme, garlic and rind in small bowl. Using a meat mallet, gently pound chicken, one piece at a time, between sheets of cling film until about 5mm thick. Divide herb mixture among chicken pieces; roll to enclose filling, wrapping each roll with a slice prosciutto of to secure.
3 Cook chicken in heated lightly oiled large frying pan, uncovered, about 10 minutes or until browned all over. Place chicken on a baking tray; cook, uncovered, in moderate oven about 15 minutes or until cooked through.
4 Meanwhile, cook tomatoes in same pan, over high heat, stirring, 3 minutes. Gently toss tomatoes, spinach and coarsely chopped basil in large bowl with combined vinegar and oil. Serve salad with chicken.

preparation time 25 minutes
cooking time 25 minutes
serves 4
per serving 7.4g fat; 1066kJ (255 cal)

Chicken dishes abound in practically every country's cuisine – and with good reason: this versatile, relatively inexpensive all-rounder tastes great in any language.

green chicken curry

750g chicken thigh fillets, sliced thinly
200g green beans, chopped coarsely
1 cup (250ml) coconut cream

green curry paste
3 fresh green thai chillies, chopped
    finely
3 spring onions, chopped finely
2 cloves garlic, crushed
¼ cup finely chopped fresh lemongrass
¼ cup chopped fresh coriander
2 tablespoons groundnut oil
2 tablespoons water
1 teaspoon shrimp paste
½ teaspoon ground cumin
¼ teaspoon ground turmeric

1 Cook green curry paste in large heated saucepan, stirring, about 3 minutes or until fragrant.
2 Add chicken and beans to pan; cook, stirring, about 5 minutes or until chicken is tender. Stir in coconut cream; simmer, uncovered, about 3 minutes or until slightly thickened. Top with sliced spring onion, if desired.

green curry paste Blend or process ingredients until smooth.

preparation time 25 minutes
cooking time 15 minutes
serves 4
per serving 30.4g fat; 1898kJ (454 cal)
tip Curry is best made just before serving. Paste can be made a week ahead and refrigerated, covered.

tandoori chicken

½ cup (140g) low-fat plain yogurt
1 tablespoon lemon juice
½ teaspoon finely grated fresh ginger
1 clove garlic, crushed
½ teaspoon caster sugar
½ teaspoon paprika
¼ teaspoon ground cumin
¼ teaspoon ground coriander
¼ teaspoon ground turmeric
pinch chilli powder
2 x 200g single chicken breast fillets

tomato and coriander salsa
1 small tomato (130g), chopped finely
½ small red onion (50g), chopped finely
1 teaspoon sugar
1 tablespoon chopped fresh coriander

1 Combine yogurt, juice, ginger, garlic, sugar, paprika and spices in large bowl. Add chicken; turn to coat in marinade. Refrigerate 3 hours or overnight.
2 Cook chicken on heated oiled grill plate, brushing with marinade, until browned both sides and tender. Serve chicken sliced thickly, with tomato and coriander salsa, and steamed rice, if desired.

tomato and coriander salsa Combine ingredients in small bowl.

preparation time 10 minutes (plus marinating time)
cooking time 15 minutes
serves 2
per serving 12.5g fat; 1457kJ (349 cal)
tip Chicken is best marinated a day ahead and refrigerated, covered.

spicy chicken wings...

teriyaki wings

24 chicken wings (approximately 2kg)
¾ cup (180ml) teriyaki sauce
2 tablespoons groundnut oil
2 teaspoons grated fresh ginger
2 cloves garlic, crushed
1 fresh red thai chilli, deseeded, chopped
  finely
1 tablespoon brown sugar
1 teaspoon sesame oil
½ teaspoon five-spice powder
1 tablespoon sesame seeds, toasted

1 Cut chicken wings into three pieces at joints;
reserve wing tips for another use.
2 Combine sauce, groundnut oil, ginger,
garlic, chilli, sugar, sesame oil and five-spice
in large bowl with chicken; toss to coat chicken
in marinade. Cover; refrigerate 3 hours or
overnight.
3 Preheat oven to hot. Drain chicken; discard
marinade. Place chicken on oiled oven rack
over baking dish; roast, uncovered, in hot oven
about 40 minutes or until browned and cooked
through, turning once.
4 Serve the chicken wings sprinkled with
sesame seeds.

per piece 4.6g fat; 268kJ (64 cal)

preparation time 15–20 minutes (plus
marinating time)
cooking time 40–45 minutes
makes 48
tips Reserved wing tips can be used to make
stock. Marinated chicken can be prepared
ahead and frozen in a sealed storage container
or freezer bag for up to 6 months.

*From left: masala-crusted chicken wings;
teriyaki chicken wings; honey-vindaloo glazed
chicken wings with garnish of rocket leaves*

honey-vindaloo wings

24 chicken wings (approximately 2kg)
⅓ cup (115g) honey
2 tablespoons vindaloo curry paste
⅓ cup (80ml) soy sauce
2 tablespoons groundnut oil

1 Cut chicken wings into three pieces at joints;
reserve wing tips for another use.
2 Combine remaining ingredients in large bowl
with chicken; toss to coat chicken in marinade.
Cover; refrigerate 3 hours or overnight.
3 Preheat oven to hot. Place undrained chicken
on oiled oven rack over baking dish; roast,
uncovered, in hot oven about 40 minutes or until
browned and cooked through, turning once.

per piece 4.5g fat; 285kJ (68 cal)

masala-crusted wings

1 tablespoon ground cumin
2 teaspoons ground coriander
1 teaspoon ground turmeric
½ teaspoon chilli powder
2 teaspoons garam masala
1 teaspoon finely grated lemon rind
2 tablespoons lemon juice
¼ cup (60ml) groundnut oil
24 chicken wings (approximately 2kg)

1 Heat medium dry frying pan; cook spices,
stirring, over low heat until fragrant. Combine
spices in large bowl with rind, juice and oil.
2 Cut chicken wings into three pieces at joints;
reserve wing tips for another use.
3 Add chicken to spice mixture; toss to coat
chicken. Cover; refrigerate 3 hours or overnight.
4 Preheat oven to hot. Place undrained chicken
on oiled oven rack over baking dish; roast,
uncovered, in hot oven about 40 minutes or until
browned and cooked through, turning once.

per piece 4.8g fat; 273kJ (65 cal)

chicken cacciatore

2 tablespoons olive oil
1.5kg chicken pieces
1 medium brown onion (150g),
　　chopped finely
1 clove garlic, crushed
½ cup (125ml) dry white wine
1½ tablespoons white wine vinegar
½ cup (125ml) chicken stock
400g can tomatoes
1 tablespoon tomato paste
1 teaspoon finely chopped fresh basil
1 teaspoon sugar
3 anchovy fillets, chopped finely
¼ cup (60ml) milk
½ cup (60g) pitted black olives, halved
2 tablespoons chopped fresh flat-leaf
　　parsley

1　Preheat oven to moderate.
2　Heat oil in large frying pan; cook chicken until browned all over. Place chicken in ovenproof dish.
3　Pour off most pan juices, leaving about 1 tablespoon in pan. Add onion and garlic to pan; cook until onion is soft. Add wine and vinegar; bring to a boil. Boil until reduced by half. Add stock; stir over high heat 2 minutes. Push tomatoes with their liquid through sieve; add to pan with paste, basil and sugar. Cook further 1 minute.
4　Pour tomato mixture over chicken pieces. Cover; cook in moderate oven 1 hour.
5　Soak anchovy in milk 5 minutes; drain on absorbent paper. Arrange chicken pieces in serving dish; keep warm. Pour pan juices into medium saucepan. Bring to a boil; boil 1 minute. Add anchovy, olive and half of the parsley to pan; cook 1 minute. Pour sauce over chicken pieces. Sprinkle with remaining parsley.

preparation time 30 minutes (plus standing time)
cooking time 1 hour 20 minutes
serves 4
per serving 42.2g fat; 2571kJ (615 cal)

honey chilli chicken

vegetable oil, for deep-frying
100g bean thread vermicelli
1 teaspoon chilli oil
3 teaspoons groundnut oil
2 medium brown onions (300g), sliced
   thinly
4 cloves garlic, crushed
1 tablespoon grated fresh ginger
1kg chicken thigh fillets, halved
½ cup (180g) honey
2 tablespoons sweet chilli sauce
500g chinese broccoli, chopped
   coarsely
¼ cup coarsely chopped fresh garlic
   chives

1 Heat vegetable oil in wok or large frying pan. Deep-fry noodles, in batches, until puffed and white; drain on absorbent paper.

2 Heat chilli oil and groundnut oil in wok or large frying pan; stir-fry onion, garlic and ginger until fragrant. Add chicken, honey and sauce; stir-fry until chicken is browned and cooked through. Add broccoli and chives; stir-fry until broccoli is just tender. Serve over noodles.

preparation time 15 minutes
cooking time 25 minutes
serves 4
per serving 27.7g fat; 2681kJ (641 cal)

char-grilled chicken with broad beans & chive butter

750g broad beans, shelled
1 tablespoon olive oil
1 small red onion (100g), sliced thinly
2 cloves garlic, crushed
2 medium tomatoes (380g), chopped
    coarsely
2 tablespoons coarsely chopped
    fresh parsley
4 single chicken breast fillets (680g)

chive butter
60g butter
2 tablespoons fresh chives

1 Boil, steam or microwave beans until tender; cool. Remove and discard grey skins.
2 Heat oil in medium frying pan; cook onion, covered, over low heat until very soft and starting to caramelise. Add garlic and beans; stir until heated through. Stir in tomato and parsley; stir over low heat 5 minutes.
3 Meanwhile, cook chicken on heated oiled grill plate (or grill or barbecue) about 5 minutes or until cooked though; turn once during cooking.
4 Serve chicken on bean mixture; top with chive butter.

chive butter Combine butter and chives together in small bowl.

preparation time 15 minutes
cooking time 20 minutes
serves 4
per serving 27g fat; 1902kJ (454 cal)

chicken osso buco

8 chicken thigh cutlets (1.3kg)
¼ cup (35g) plain flour
2 tablespoons olive oil
1 large leek (500g), sliced thickly
2 cloves garlic, crushed
2 tablespoons tomato paste
2½ cups (625ml) chicken stock
½ cup (125ml) dry white wine
400g canned tomatoes
3 trimmed sticks celery (225g),
    chopped coarsely
2 medium carrots (240g), chopped

gremolata
1 medium lemon (140g)
¼ cup finely chopped fresh parsley
2 cloves garlic, chopped finely

preparation time 25 minutes
cooking time 1 hour 45 minutes
serves 4
per serving 15.6g fat; 1971kJ
(471 cal)

1 Remove and discard skin from chicken. Reserve
1 tablespoon of the flour. Toss chicken in remaining
flour; shake off excess. Heat half of the oil in large
saucepan; cook chicken, in batches, until browned
all over.
2 Heat remaining oil in pan; cook leek and garlic,
stirring, until leek is soft. Add reserved flour and
paste; cook, stirring, 1 minute. Stir in stock, wine and
undrained crushed tomatoes; bring to a boil.
3 Return chicken to pan. Reduce heat; simmer,
covered, 1¼ hours. Add celery and carrot; simmer,
uncovered, 20 minutes or until vegetables are soft.
4 Just before serving, sprinkle with gremolata.

gremolata Using vegetable peeler, remove rind from
lemon. Cut rind into thin strips; chop finely. Combine
lemon, parsley and garlic in small bowl; mix well.

cajun chicken & tomato salsa

750g chicken breast fillets, sliced thinly
¼ cup (18g) cajun seasoning
2 teaspoons grated lime rind
2 trimmed corn cobs (500g)
2 tablespoons olive oil
1 small red onion (100g), cut into thin
   wedges

tomato salsa
2 small plum tomatoes (120g),
   chopped finely
2 spring onions, sliced thinly
2 teaspoons lime juice
2 teaspoons balsamic vinegar

1 Combine chicken, seasoning and rind in large bowl; mix well. Cut kernels from corn.
2 Heat half of the oil in wok or large frying pan; stir-fry chicken mixture, in batches, until cooked through.
3 Heat remaining oil in wok; stir-fry corn and onion until onion is soft.
4 Return chicken to wok; stir-fry until hot.
5 Serve chicken mixture topped with tomato salsa.

tomato salsa Combine ingredients in small bowl; mix well.

preparation time 20 minutes
cooking time 15 minutes
serves 4
per serving 21.2g fat; 1877kJ (449 cal)
tip Recipe best made just before serving; serve with sour cream, if desired.

moroccan chicken with beetroot purée & couscous

8 single chicken breast fillets (1.4kg)
1 tablespoon olive oil
2 teaspoons finely grated lemon rind
2 tablespoons lemon juice
2 cloves garlic, crushed
1 tablespoon ground coriander
1 tablespoon ground cumin
2 teaspoons ground cardamom
1 teaspoon sweet paprika
1 teaspoon ground turmeric
½ cup chopped fresh flat-leaf parsley
¼ cup chopped fresh coriander
2 cups (400g) couscous
2 cups (500ml) boiling water
¼ cup chopped fresh mint

beetroot purée
6 medium beetroot (1kg), trimmed
½ cup (140g) low-fat plain yogurt

----

preparation time 30 minutes (plus marinating time)
cooking time 1 hour
serves 8
per serving 13g fat; 2133kJ (510 cal)
tip Cardamom pods should be bruised with the side of a heavy knife until crushed just to the point of opening; the seeds can then be extracted and used, whole or ground.

----

1 Combine chicken, oil, rind, juice, garlic, spices, parsley and fresh coriander in large bowl. Cover; marinate in refrigerator 1 hour.
2 Prepare beetroot puree.
3 Combine couscous and the water in large heatproof bowl. Cover; stand for 5 minutes or until the water is absorbed, fluffing couscous with fork occasionally to separate grains. Add mint; toss gently to combine.
4 Cook undrained chicken, in batches, in large heated lightly oiled non-stick frying pan until browned both sides and cooked through. Slice chicken and serve on couscous; top with beetroot puree.

beetroot purée Preheat oven to moderate. Wrap unpeeled beetroot in foil. Place on oven tray; roast in moderate oven about 1 hour or until tender. When cool enough to handle, peel beetroot; chop coarsely. Blend or process beetroot until pureed. Stir in yogurt; cover to keep warm.

meat

beef & rice noodle stir-fry

500g fresh rice noodles
2 tablespoons groundnut oil
500g beef fillets, sliced thinly
1 clove garlic, crushed
1 tablespoon grated fresh ginger
1 tablespoon finely chopped fresh
    lemongrass
1 fresh red thai chilli, deseeded,
    chopped finely
1 tablespoon chopped fresh mint
1 large carrot (180g), halved
    lengthways, sliced thinly
200g fresh baby corn, halved
    lengthways
200g chinese broccoli, chopped
    coarsely
1 tablespoon brown sugar
2 teaspoons cornflour
¼ cup (60ml) rice wine
¼ cup (60ml) oyster sauce
2 tablespoons light soy sauce

1 Rinse noodles under hot water; drain. Transfer to large bowl; separate noodles with fork.
2 Heat half of the oil in wok or large frying pan; stir-fry beef, in batches, until browned all over.
3 Heat remaining oil in wok; stir-fry garlic, ginger, lemongrass, chilli and mint until fragrant. Add carrot and corn; stir-fry until carrot is just tender.
4 Return beef to wok with broccoli, sugar and blended cornflour, wine and sauces; stir-fry until broccoli just wilts and sauce boils and thickens slightly. Add noodles; stir-fry until hot.

preparation time 15 minutes
cooking time 20 minutes
serves 4
per serving 16.5g fat; 2011kJ (481 cal)
tip Fresh rice noodles must be rinsed under hot water to remove starch and excess oil before using. You can substitute egg noodles for the rice noodles.

From traditional cassoulet to tasty meatballs in chilli mushroom sauce and spicy harissa lamb with char-grilled vegetables, here are some creative beef, lamb, pork and veal dishes for you to try.

beef & vegetables with herb pesto

1 tablespoon olive oil
400g beef steak, sliced thinly
1 clove garlic, crushed
20 baby carrots, halved lengthways
1 medium red pepper (200g), chopped
    coarsely
1 medium yellow pepper (200g),
    chopped coarsely
200g sugar snap peas
½ cup (125ml) beef stock

herb pesto
1½ cups firmly packed fresh basil leaves
¼ cup firmly packed fresh oregano
⅓ cup (25g) grated parmesan
¼ cup (60ml) olive oil
¼ cup (60ml) double cream
1 clove garlic, crushed
1 tablespoon balsamic vinegar
2 teaspoons water

1 Heat oil in wok or large frying pan. Stir-fry beef and garlic, in batches, until beef is browned.
2 Stir-fry carrot and pepper.
3 Return beef mixture to wok with peas and stock; stir until hot.
4 Serve stir-fry topped with warm herb pesto.

herb pesto Blend or process herbs, cheese, oil, cream, garlic, vinegar and the water until combined. Transfer mixture to small saucepan; stir over low heat, without boiling, until heated through.

preparation time 25 minutes
cooking time 15 minutes
serves 4
per serving 31.9g fat; 1893kJ (453 cal)

braised beef curry with dhal

1 tablespoon groundnut oil

2 medium brown onions (300g), chopped coarsely

2 cloves garlic, crushed

1 fresh red thai chilli, chopped finely

1 tablespoon grated fresh ginger

2 teaspoons garam masala

2 tablespoons ground cumin

2 tablespoons ground coriander

2 teaspoons hot paprika

4 cardamom pods, bruised

3 cinnamon sticks, broken

2 cups (500ml) water

2kg beef chuck steak, cut into 2cm pieces

3 cups (750ml) beef stock

½ cup (125ml) coconut milk

⅓ cup chopped fresh coriander

3 cups (600g) red lentils

1 Heat oil in large heavy-based saucepan; cook onion, garlic, chilli and ginger, stirring, until onion is soft. Stir in spices; cook, stirring, until fragrant.

2 Gradually stir ¼ cup (60ml) of the water into onion mixture until it forms a paste; cook, stirring, 2 minutes. Add beef; stir to coat in paste.

3 Add the remaining water and stock; bring to a boil. Reduce heat; simmer, covered, stirring occasionally, about 1½ hours or until beef is tender. Refrigerate overnight, to allow flavours to develop.

4 Add coconut milk; simmer, uncovered, about 30 minutes or until thickened slightly. Discard cardamom pods and cinnamon sticks. Stir in coriander.

5 Meanwhile, cook lentils in medium saucepan of boiling water, uncovered, about 10 minutes or until tender; drain. Serve lentils with curry.

preparation time 15 minutes (plus refrigeration time)
cooking time 2 hours 30 minutes
serves 8
per serving 20.1g fat; 2516kJ (602 cal)

veal parmesan

4 veal steaks (320g)
plain flour
1 egg
1 tablespoon water
packaged breadcrumbs
30g butter
⅓ cup (80ml) olive oil
2½ cups (250g) grated mozzarella
¾ cup (60g) grated parmesan

tomato sauce
1 tablespoon olive oil
1 medium brown onion (150g),
 chopped finely
1 trimmed stick celery (75g), chopped
 finely
1 medium red pepper (200g), chopped
 finely
1 clove garlic, crushed
410g canned tomatoes
2 teaspoons sugar
1 tablespoon tomato paste
1½ cups (375ml) chicken stock
1 tablespoon finely chopped fresh
 parsley
1 tablespoon finely chopped fresh basil

1 Pound veal out thinly. Toss veal in flour; shake off excess. Dip in combined beaten egg and water; press on breadcrumbs. Refrigerate veal while preparing tomato sauce.

2 Heat butter and half of the oil in large frying pan; cook veal until browned both sides. Place in ovenproof dish; top veal with mozzarella. Spoon tomato sauce over mozzarella.

3 Sprinkle evenly with parmesan; drizzle with remaining oil. Bake uncovered in moderate oven about 20 minutes or until golden brown.

tomato sauce Heat oil in medium frying pan; cook onion, celery, pepper and garlic, stirring until onion is soft. Push tomatoes with their liquid through sieve. Add pureed tomato to pan with sugar, paste and stock. Cover; bring to a boil. Reduce heat; simmer, covered, 30 minutes. Remove lid; simmer until sauce is thick. Stir through parsley and basil.

preparation time 35 minutes
cooking time 1 hour 20 minutes
serves 4
per serving 52.8g fat; 3316kJ (792 cal)

pepper steaks with balsamic browned onions

1 teaspoon cracked black pepper
2 tablespoons finely chopped fresh
   parsley
4 beef sirloin steaks (800g)
¼ cup (60ml) olive oil
2 large onions (400g), sliced thinly
2 tablespoons balsamic vinegar
1 tablespoon drained, chopped
   sun-dried tomatoes in oil
2 cloves garlic, crushed

1 Press pepper and parsley onto beef; stand, covered, while cooking onions.

2 Heat 1 tablespoon of the oil in large frying pan; cook onions, stirring, about 10 minutes or until just browned. Add 1 tablespoon of the vinegar; cook, stirring, further 5 minutes or until onion caramelises. Remove from pan; cover to keep warm. Combine remaining oil and vinegar in small screw-top jar with tomatoes and garlic; shake well.

3 Cook beef on heated oiled grill plate (or grill or barbecue) until browned both sides and cooked as desired. Serve beef with browned onions and tomato dressing.

preparation time 10 minutes
cooking time 20 minutes
serves 4
per serving 28g fat; 1887kJ (451 cal)

meatballs with chilli mushroom sauce

500g minced beef or veal
1 cup (70g) stale breadcrumbs
¼ cup finely chopped fresh oregano
3 cloves garlic, crushed
⅓ cup (95g) tomato paste
1 egg, beaten lightly
1 tablespoon olive oil
250g button mushrooms, sliced thinly
850g canned tomatoes
¼ cup (60ml) mild chilli sauce

1 Combine mince, breadcrumbs, oregano, garlic, paste and egg in medium bowl; roll level tablespoons of mixture into balls. Place meatballs on oiled baking tray; bake, uncovered, in moderately hot oven about 15 minutes or until cooked through.
2 Meanwhile, heat oil in large saucepan; cook mushrooms, stirring, until just soft. Add undrained crushed tomatoes and sauce to pan; bring to a boil. Reduce heat; simmer, uncovered, 5 minutes. Add meatballs; cook, stirring, 2 minutes.

preparation time 15 minutes
cooking time 20 minutes
serves 4
per serving 16.4g fat; 1649kJ (394 cal)
tip Recipe can be made 2 days ahead and refrigerated, covered, or frozen for up to 3 months.

braised pork with fresh sage

90g butter
1.5kg rack of pork (6 cutlets)
2 medium carrots (240g), sliced thickly
6 baby onions (150g), peeled
4 cloves garlic, peeled
2 bay leaves
6 sprigs fresh thyme
1⅓ cups (330ml) dry white wine

fresh sage sauce
15g butter
1 tablespoon plain flour
1 tablespoon fresh sage

1 Melt butter in large flameproof dish; cook rack of pork until browned each side. Remove pork from dish.
2 Place carrot, onion, garlic, bay leaves and thyme in dish; stir over heat about 5 minutes or until just browned. Return pork to dish with wine; transfer to moderate oven about 1¼ hours or until tender. Remove pork; keep warm.
3 Strain cooking liquid; reserve liquid. Discard the vegetables.
4 Serve pork with sage sauce, roasted tomatoes and potatoes, if desired.

fresh sage sauce Bring reserved liquid to a boil in medium saucepan; whisk in blended butter and flour. Boil, whisking constantly, until thickened slightly; stir in sage.

preparation time 15 minutes
cooking time 1 hour 30 minutes
serves 6
per serving 35.6g fat; 2052kJ (490 cal)
tips Ask your butcher to remove rind and tie pork well. Roast salted rind on rack in hot oven until crisp; serve with the pork.

pork steaks & baked peppers

4 pork butterfly steaks (600g)
¼ teaspoon cracked black pepper
½ teaspoon dried oregano
2 teaspoons olive oil
1 teaspoon cornflour
1 cup (250ml) chicken stock
2 teaspoons red wine vinegar

baked peppers
2 medium yellow peppers (400g)
2 large plum tomatoes (180g), halved
90g button mushrooms, sliced thinly
4 cloves garlic, crushed
¼ teaspoon dried oregano
2 teaspoons olive oil
16 pitted black olives (80g)
2 tablespoons grated parmesan

preparation time 20 minutes
cooking time 1 hour 10 minutes
serves 4
per serving 11.7g fat; 1239kJ
(296 cal)
tip Recipe can be made a day
ahead and refrigerated, covered.

1   Sprinkle pork with pepper and oregano. Heat oil in large frying pan; cook pork, until tender, turning once. Remove from pan.
2   Add blended cornflour and stock to pan; stir until mixture boils and thickens. Add vinegar; return pork to pan. Turn to coat in sauce.
3   Serve with baked pepper salad. Sprinkle with fresh oregano, if desired.

baked peppers Quarter peppers; remove seeds and membranes. Place pepper on oiled baking tray with tomato, mushrooms and garlic; sprinkle with oregano and oil. Bake, uncovered, in moderately hot oven 40 minutes. Add olives; sprinkle cheese over tomato. Bake further 15 minutes or until peppers are tender.

harissa-scented lamb with char-grilled vegetables

Harissa, a Moroccan sauce or paste made from dried red chillies, garlic oil and caraway seeds, can be used as a rub for meat, an ingredient in sauces and dressings, or eaten on its own as a condiment. It is available commercially from supermarkets.

3 cloves garlic, crushed
1 tablespoon finely grated lemon rind
2 tablespoons harissa
⅓ cup (80ml) lemon juice
1.5kg butterflied leg of lamb, trimmed
2 medium red peppers (400g), sliced thickly
3 large courgettes (450g), sliced thickly
8 baby aubergines (480g), sliced thickly
1 teaspoon ground cumin
1 tablespoon fresh thyme leaves
½ cup coarsely chopped fresh mint

garlic sauce
1 clove garlic, crushed
1 teaspoon ground cumin
½ cup (125ml) buttermilk
⅓ cup (95g) low-fat plain yogurt

1 Make garlic sauce.
2 Combine crushed garlic, rind, harissa and half of the juice in large bowl, add lamb; toss lamb to coat in mixture.
3 Cook lamb on heated lightly oiled grill plate (or grill or barbecue), covered, about 20 minutes or until lamb is cooked as desired. Cover lamb; stand 5 minutes before slicing thickly.
4 Meanwhile, combine pepper, courgettes, aubergine, cumin and remaining juice in large bowl. Cook vegetables on same grill plate (or grill or barbecue) until just tender. Return vegetables to bowl with herbs; toss gently to combine.
5 Serve lamb with char-grilled vegetables; drizzle with garlic sauce.

garlic sauce Combine all ingredients in screw-top jar; shake well.

preparation time 20 minutes
cooking time 30 minutes
serves 6
per serving 7g fat; 1780kJ (354 cal)

chilli coriander lamb with barley salad

1 tablespoon coriander seeds, crushed lightly
½ teaspoon dried chilli flakes
2 cloves garlic, crushed
4 loins of lamb (800g)
1 cup (200g) pearl barley
¼ teaspoon ground turmeric
⅓ cup coarsely chopped fresh mint
⅓ cup coarsely chopped fresh coriander
1 small red onion (100g), chopped finely
250g cherry tomatoes, quartered
¼ cup (60ml) lemon juice
2 teaspoons olive oil

1 Combine seeds, chilli and garlic in medium bowl, add lamb; toss lamb to coat in mixture. Cover; refrigerate until required.
2 Meanwhile, cook barley in large saucepan of boiling water, uncovered, about 20 minutes or until just tender; drain. Rinse under cold water; drain.
3 Cook lamb on heated lightly oiled grill plate (or grill or barbecue) until cooked as desired. Cover lamb; stand 5 minutes before slicing thickly.
4 Combine remaining ingredients in large bowl, add barley; toss gently to combine. Serve salad with lamb.

preparation time 20 minutes
cooking time 30 minutes
serves 4
per serving 10.9g fat; 1822kJ (436 cal)

lamb & lentil curry

1 cup (200g) yellow split peas
1 tablespoon olive oil
600g lamb fillets, diced into 4cm
    pieces
2 large brown onions (400g), sliced
    thinly
5cm piece fresh ginger (25g), chopped
    finely
2 cloves garlic, crushed
2 tablespoons ground coriander
1 tablespoon sweet paprika
½ teaspoon cayenne pepper
200g plain yogurt
2 medium tomatoes (300g), chopped
    coarsely
1¾ cups (430ml) chicken stock
⅔ cup (160ml) light coconut cream
150g baby spinach leaves
⅓ cup coarsely chopped fresh
    coriander

1 Cook split peas in medium saucepan of boiling water, uncovered, until just tender; drain.
2 Meanwhile, heat half of the oil in large saucepan; cook lamb, in batches, stirring, until cooked as desired. Drain on absorbent paper.
3 Heat remaining oil in same pan; cook onion, stirring, about 15 minutes until caramelised. Add ginger, garlic and spices; cook, stirring, until fragrant. Add yogurt; cook 5 minutes, without boiling, stirring.
4 Add tomato, stock and coconut cream; bring to a boil. Reduce heat; simmer, uncovered, 15 minutes or until sauce thickens slightly. Return lamb to pan with split peas and spinach; cook, stirring, until heated through. Remove from heat; stir in fresh coriander.

preparation time 15 minutes
cooking time 55 minutes
serves 4
per serving 19.3g fat; 2153kJ (515 cal)

lamb madras curry

500g butternut squash, diced into 2cm
  pieces
200g green beans, chopped coarsely
2 tablespoons vegetable oil
600g loin of lamb, diced into 2cm
  pieces
1 medium brown onion (150g),
  chopped finely
2 cloves garlic, crushed
½ cup (150g) madras curry paste
1 cup (250ml) beef stock
425g can crushed tomatoes
2 cups (400g) basmati rice
1 cup (250ml) buttermilk
½ cup coarsely chopped fresh
  coriander

1 Boil, steam or microwave squash and beans, separately, until just tender; drain. Rinse beans under cold water; drain.
2 Meanwhile, heat half of the oil in wok; stir-fry lamb, in batches, until just browned.
3 Heat remaining oil in same wok; stir-fry onion and garlic until onion softens. Add paste; stir-fry until fragrant. Return lamb to wok with stock and undrained tomatoes; bring to a boil. Add squash, reduce heat; simmer curry, covered, stirring occasionally, 10 minutes.
4 Meanwhile, cook rice in large saucepan of boiling water, uncovered, until just tender; drain.
5 Add beans and buttermilk to curry; stir over low heat until heated through. Remove from heat; stir in coriander. Serve curry with rice, sprinkle with extra chopped fresh corriander, if desired.

preparation time 10 minutes
cooking time 30 minutes
serves 4
per serving 36.9g fat; 3829kJ
(916 cal)

mongolian lamb stir-fry

1½ cups (300g) white long-grain rice
2 tablespoons groundnut oil
600g lamb strips
2 cloves garlic, crushed
1cm piece fresh ginger (5g), grated
1 medium brown onion (150g), sliced
    thickly
1 medium red pepper (200g), sliced
    thickly
230g can bamboo shoots, rinsed,
    drained
¼ cup (60ml) soy sauce
1 tablespoon black bean sauce
1 tablespoon cornflour
2 tablespoons rice wine vinegar
6 spring onions, cut into 5cm lengths

1 Cook rice in large saucepan of boiling water, uncovered, until just tender; drain. Cover to keep warm.
2 Meanwhile, heat half of the oil in wok; stir-fry lamb, in batches, until browned all over.
3 Heat remaining oil in same wok; stir-fry garlic, ginger and brown onion until onion softens. Add pepper and bamboo shoots; stir-fry until vegetables are just tender. Return lamb to wok with sauces and blended cornflour and vinegar; stir-fry until sauce boils and thickens slightly. Remove from heat; stir in spring onion.
4 Serve stir-fry with warm rice.

preparation time 15 minutes
cooking time 20 minutes
serves 4
per serving 23.2g fat; 2709kJ
(648 cal)

cassoulet

There are many regional variations of French cassoulet, and ours is based on a traditional Toulousaine version which traditionally calls for mutton. We used dried white haricot beans in this recipe, but cannellini or butterbeans can be used if you prefer.

1 cup (200g) dried white beans
150g piece streaky bacon, rind
    removed, diced into 1cm pieces
500g thin lamb sausages, sliced thickly
1 medium brown onion (150g),
    chopped finely
2 trimmed celery stalks (200g),
    chopped finely
2 cloves garlic, crushed
1 sprig fresh rosemary
2 bay leaves
425g can crushed tomatoes
1½ cups (375ml) chicken stock
2 cups (140g) stale breadcrumbs
⅓ cup coarsely chopped fresh flat-leaf
    parsley

herb and rocket salad
60g baby rocket leaves
1 cup loosely packed fresh flat-leaf
    parsley leaves
1 cup loosely packed fresh chervil
    sprigs
½ cup loosely packed fresh basil leaves
¼ cup (60ml) olive oil
2 tablespoons red wine vinegar
1 teaspoon white sugar

1 Place beans in large bowl, cover with water; soak overnight, drain. Rinse under cold water; drain. Place beans in medium saucepan covered with boiling water; bring to a boil. Reduce heat; simmer, covered, about 15 minutes or until beans are just tender. Drain.
2 Preheat oven to moderately low (160°C/140°C fan-assisted).
3 Cook bacon in large flameproof casserole dish over high heat, pressing down with back of spoon, until browned all over; remove from dish. Cook sausages in same dish until browned all over; remove from dish.
4 Cook onion, celery and garlic in same dish, stirring, about 5 minutes or until soft. Add rosemary, bay leaves, undrained tomatoes, stock, beans, bacon and sausage; bring to a boil. Cover; cook in moderately low oven 30 minutes. Remove from oven; sprinkle with combined breadcrumbs and parsley. Return to oven; cook, covered, 30 minutes. Uncover; cook about 10 minutes or until top browns lightly.
5 Meanwhile, make herb and rocket salad. Toss salad with vinaigrette just before serving with cassoulet.

herb and rocket salad Combine rocket, parsley, chervil and basil in large bowl. Place remaining ingredients in screw-top jar; shake vinaigrette well.

preparation time 40 minutes (plus standing time)
cooking time 1 hour 40 minutes
serves 4
per serving 44.3g fat; 3603kJ (862 cal)

marinated lamb with caponata & lemon thyme polenta

Caponata, a classic Sicilian aubergine and pepper dish, is usually eaten at room temperature as part of an antipasti or as a relish accompanying a roast, as we suggest here.

2kg leg of lamb
2 teaspoons sweet paprika
¼ cup (60ml) lemon juice
1 tablespoon olive oil
2 cloves garlic, crushed
3 cups (750ml) beef stock
2 teaspoons finely shredded lemon rind
2 tablespoons coarsely chopped fresh
    lemon thyme

caponata
2 tablespoons olive oil
6 baby aubergines (360g), chopped
    coarsely
2 medium brown onions (300g),
    chopped coarsely
3 cloves garlic, crushed
2 trimmed celery stalks (200g),
    chopped coarsely
2 medium red peppers (400g),
    chopped coarsely
1 tablespoon baby capers, rinsed,
    drained
2 tablespoons red wine vinegar
3 large plum tomatoes (270g), chopped
    coarsely
½ cup coarsely chopped fresh basil
¼ cup (40g) toasted pine nuts

lemon thyme polenta
2 cups (500ml) water
2½ cups (625ml) milk
1 cup (170g) polenta
½ cup (40g) finely grated parmesan
1 tablespoon fresh lemon thyme leaves

1 Using sharp knife, pierce lamb all over; place in large bowl. Rub combined paprika, juice, oil and garlic all over lamb, pressing into cuts. Cover; refrigerate 3 hours or overnight.
2 Preheat oven to moderately hot (200°C/180°C fan-assisted).
3 Pour stock into large shallow baking dish; place lamb on wire rack over dish, drizzle with any remaining paprika mixture. Roast, uncovered, in moderately hot oven 30 minutes, brushing lamb occasionally with pan juices. Reduce heat to moderate (180°C/160°C fan-assisted); roast, uncovered, about 1 hour and 15 minutes or until lamb is cooked as desired. Cover lamb; stand 20 minutes.
4 Meanwhile, make caponata. Make lemon thyme polenta.
5 Serve sliced lamb, sprinkled with combined rind and thyme, with caponata and polenta.

caponata Heat half of the oil in large saucepan; cook aubergine until browned all over. Remove from pan. Heat remaining oil in same pan; cook onion, stirring, until soft. Add garlic, celery and pepper; cook, stirring, until vegetables soften. Stir in capers, vinegar, tomato, aubergine and half of the basil; cook, covered, over low heat about 15 minutes or until mixture thickens slightly. Stir remaining basil and pine nuts into caponata just before serving.

lemon thyme polenta Combine the water and milk in large saucepan; bring to a boil. Gradually add polenta, stirring constantly. Reduce heat; cook, stirring, about 10 minutes or until polenta thickens. Stir in cheese and lemon thyme.

preparation time 30 minutes (plus refrigerationtime)
cooking time 1 hour 45 minutes (plus standing time)
serves 4
per serving 52g fat; 4544kJ (1087 cal)

lamb chops with creamy mash & flavoured butter

Make any one of the following three flavoured butter accompaniments to melt on your chops and serve with our yummy mashed potatoes.

4 large potatoes (1.2kg), chopped
   coarsely
50g butter
½ cup (120g) soured cream
8 lamb loin chops (800g)

preparation time 25 minutes
cooking time 30 minutes
serves 4
per serving (without butter) 35.5g fat;
2587kJ (619 cal)

1   Make the flavoured butter of your choice (see opposite).
2   Meanwhile, boil, steam or microwave potato until tender; drain. Mash potato in large bowl with butter and soured cream until smooth; cover to keep warm.
3   Cook lamb on heated oiled grill plate (or grill or barbecue) until browned both sides and cooked as desired. Serve lamb with the creamy mash and your chosen butter.

parsley & rosemary butter

1 tablespoon finely chopped fresh
  flat-leaf parsley
2 tablespoons finely chopped fresh
  rosemary
80g butter, softened

1 Blend or process ingredients until smooth.
Place on piece of cling film; shape into a rectangular
block.
2 Wrap butter mixture tightly in plastic wrap. Freeze
until just firm; remove 10 minutes before serving.

per serving (butter only) 16.4g fat; 610kJ (146 cal)

roast garlic & chilli butter

6 cloves garlic, unpeeled
1 fresh small red thai chilli, chopped
  finely
80g butter, softened

1 Preheat oven to moderately hot (200°C/180°C
fan-assisted).
2 Roast garlic in small baking dish, uncovered, in
moderately hot oven about 15 minutes or until garlic
is tender.
3 When cool enough to handle, peel garlic. Blend or
process garlic, chilli and butter until smooth. Place on
piece of cling film; shape into a rectangular block.
4 Wrap butter mixture tightly in plastic wrap. Freeze
until just firm; remove 10 minutes before serving.

per serving (butter only) 16.5g fat; 627kJ (150 cal)

lemon & pepper butter

2 teaspoons finely grated lemon rind
1 tablespoon lemon juice
1 tablespoon cracked black pepper
80g butter, softened

1 Blend or process ingredients until smooth. Place
on piece of cling film; shape into a rectangular block.
2 Wrap butter mixture tightly in plastic wrap. Freeze
until just firm; remove 10 minutes before serving.

per serving (butter only) 16.5g fat; 635kJ (150 cal)

layered vine leaves with aubergine & lamb

Baharat, an aromatic all-purpose spice blend, can be made with some or all of the following: mixed spice, black pepper, allspice, dried chilli flakes, paprika, coriander seeds, cinnamon, clove, sumac, nutmeg, cumin seeds and cardamom seeds. It is used throughout the Middle East; here, it is often sold as lebanese seven-spice, and can be found at Middle-Eastern food stores, some delicatessens and specialist food shops.

2 large red peppers (700g)
1 medium aubergine (300g), cut crossways into 12 slices
1 medium brown onion (150g), chopped finely
1 clove garlic, crushed
500g minced lamb
2 teaspoons baharat
1 tablespoon brandy
1 tablespoon tomato paste
½ cup (125ml) beef stock
1 tablespoon lime juice
1 tablespoon toasted pine nuts
1 cup coarsely chopped fresh flat-leaf parsley
8 fresh vine leaves (or use cabbage leaves if preferred)

1 Quarter peppers; remove seeds and membrane. Place pepper, skin-side up, and aubergine on lightly oiled oven tray under preheated grill or in preheated hot oven until skin blisters. Cover pepper with cling film or paper for 5 minutes; peel away skin, then slice the flesh thinly.

2 Meanwhile, cook onion and garlic in heated lightly oiled large frying pan, stirring, until onion just softens. Add mince and spice; cook, stirring, until mince changes colour. Stir in combined brandy, paste and stock; bring to a boil. Reduce heat; simmer, uncovered, stirring, about 2 minutes or until liquid reduces by half. Remove from heat; stir in juice, nuts and parsley. Cover to keep warm.

3 Place vine leaves in large saucepan of boiling water, uncovered, for about 30 seconds or just until pliable; drain, in single layer, on absorbent paper.

4 Place one leaf on each plate; layer each leaf with one slice of aubergine, a few pepper slices, ¼ cup mince mixture and another vine leaf. Repeat layering with remaining aubergine, pepper and mince.

preparation time 20 minutes
cooking time 20 minutes
serves 4
per serving 15.5g fat; 1321kJ (316 cal)
tips Make a substitute for baharat by combining 2 teaspoons paprika, 1 tablespoon ground cumin, 1 tablespoon ground coriander, 1 crushed clove and ½ teaspoon ground nutmeg.
If fresh vine leaves are unavailable, buy those vacuum-packed and preserved in brine. Rinse thoroughly under cold water, then follow step 3 above, reducing time in the boiling water to 10 seconds.

prawns with chilli, coriander & lime butter

16 large uncooked king prawns
100g butter, melted
2 fresh red thai chillies, deseeded, chopped finely
2 tablespoons lime juice
2 tablespoons finely chopped fresh coriander
50g mixed baby salad leaves

1 Shell prawns, leaving tails intact. To butterfly prawns, cut halfway through the back of each prawn. Remove veins; press flat.
2 Cook prawns on heated oiled grill pan or in heavy-base frying pan until changed in colour and just cooked through.
3 Meanwhile, combine butter, chilli, juice and coriander in medium bowl.
4 Serve mixed salad leaves with prawns, drizzled with hot butter mixture.

preparation time 10 minutes
cooking time 5 minutes
serves 4
per serving 21.2g fat; 1153kJ (275 cal)

garlic prawns & pak choy with herbed rice

36 medium uncooked prawns (1kg)
6 cloves garlic, crushed
3 fresh red thai chillies, deseeded, chopped finely
2 teaspoons finely chopped fresh coriander
⅓ cup (80ml) lime juice
1 teaspoon sugar
1 tablespoon groundnut oil
1kg baby pak choy, quartered lengthways
6 spring onions, sliced thinly
1 tablespoon sweet chilli sauce

herbed rice
2 cups (400g) jasmine rice
2 tablespoons chopped fresh coriander
1 tablespoon chopped fresh mint
1 tablespoon chopped fresh flat-leaf parsley
1 teaspoon finely grated lime rind

1 Shell and devein prawns, leaving tails intact.
2 Combine prawns in large bowl with garlic, chilli, coriander, juice and sugar.
3 Heat half of the oil in wok or large non-stick frying pan; stir-fry prawns, in batches, until just changed in colour.
4 Heat remaining oil with pan liquids in wok; stir-fry pak choy, onion and sauce, in batches, until just tender. Combine pak choy mixture and prawns in wok; stir-fry until hot. Serve prawns on herbed rice.

herbed rice Cook rice, uncovered, in large saucepan of boiling water until tender; drain. Return rice to pan; combine with remaining ingredients.

preparation time 20 minutes
cooking time 15 minutes
serves 6
per serving 4.5g fat; 1602kJ (383 cal)

slow-roasted salmon with asian greens

750g piece salmon fillet, boned, skin left on
1 fresh kaffir lime, quartered
1 tablespoon finely shredded kaffir lime leaves
1 tablespoon groundnut oil
250g fresh asparagus, trimmed, chopped coarsely
150g mangetout
150g baby pak choy, chopped coarsely
150g choy sum, chopped coarsely

chilli sauce
½ cup (110g) caster sugar
¼ cup (60ml) lime juice
¼ cup (60ml) water
2 fresh red thai chillies, deseeded, chopped finely
¼ cup firmly packed fresh coriander

1 Preheat oven to very low.
2 Cook fish and lime on heated oiled grill plate (or grill or barbecue) until both are lightly coloured all over. Place fish and lime in large oiled baking dish; sprinkle with lime leaves. Bake, covered tightly, in very slow oven about 30 minutes or until cooked as desired.
3 Heat oil in wok or large frying pan; stir-fry asparagus and mangetout until just tender. Add pak choy and choy sum with half of the chilli sauce; stir-fry until leaves are just wilted.
4 Serve vegetables with fish, drizzled with remaining chilli sauce.

chilli sauce Combine sugar, juice and the water in small saucepan; stir over heat, without boiling, until sugar dissolves. Simmer, uncovered, without stirring, 3 minutes; cool slightly. Stir in chilli and coriander.

preparation time 15 minutes
cooking time 40 minutes
serves 4
per serving 16.3g fat; 1686kJ (403 cal)

fish cutlets with caper & herb crust

1 cup (155g) pine nuts
¼ cup (40g) rolled oats
¼ cup (35g) white sesame seeds
2 cups (200g) packaged breadcrumbs
½ teaspoon mustard powder
1 tablespoon grated lemon rind
1 tablespoon lemon juice
1 egg, beaten lightly
1 tablespoon honey
2 tablespoons chopped fresh parsley
2 tablespoons chopped fresh lemon thyme
2 tablespoons drained capers, chopped coarsely
1 cup (80g) grated parmesan
8 firm white fish cutlets (1.5kg)
plain flour
2 eggs, beaten lightly, extra
½ cup (125ml) vegetable oil

1 Process pine nuts, oats and seeds until chopped finely; transfer to large bowl. Stir in breadcrumbs, mustard, rind, juice, egg, honey, herbs, capers and cheese; mix well.

2 Toss fish in flour; shake away excess. Dip fish in extra egg, then in breadcrumb mixture.

3 Heat oil in large frying pan; cook fish, in batches, until browned lightly both sides. Transfer to large baking tray; bake, uncovered, in moderate oven about 15 minutes or until cutlets are tender.

4 Serve with lemon wedges and asparagus spears, if desired.

preparation time 20 minutes
cooking time 20 minutes
serves 8
per serving 40.3g fat; 2687kJ (642 cal)

fish kebabs with almond & lemon couscous

½ cup finely chopped fresh coriander

2 cloves garlic, crushed

2 tablespoons olive oil

2 fresh small red thai chillies, chopped finely

¼ cup (60ml) lemon juice

800g skinless fish fillets, diced into 3cm pieces

1½ cups (375ml) chicken stock

1½ cups (300g) couscous

½ cup firmly packed fresh coriander leaves

1 tablespoon finely chopped preserved lemon

¼ cup (35g) toasted slivered almonds

1 Combine chopped coriander, garlic, oil, chilli and juice in small bowl. Place half of the coriander mixture in large bowl, add fish; toss fish to coat in mixture. Thread fish onto skewers; place kebabs on tray. Cover; refrigerate 45 minutes.

2 Cook kebabs on heated lightly oiled grill plate (or grill or barbecue) about 5 minutes or until cooked as desired.

3 Meanwhile, bring stock to a boil in small saucepan; remove from heat. Add couscous to stock, cover; stand about 5 minutes or until liquid is absorbed, fluffing with fork occasionally. Add remaining coriander mixture, coriander leaves, lemon and nuts; toss gently to combine. Serve couscous with kebabs.

preparation time 25 minutes (plus refrigeration time)
cooking time 10 minutes serves 4
per serving 16g fat; 2391kJ (572 cal)
tips You will need to soak eight 25cm bamboo skewers in water for at least an hour before using to prevent them from splintering or scorching.
You can use any firm white-fleshed fish fillets for this recipe.

fish fillets with garlic & chilli dressing

¼ cup (60ml) olive oil
4 fish fillets (800g), skin left on
   (any firm-fleshed white fish
   is suitable)
1 clove garlic, crushed
1½ tablespoons sherry vinegar
1 teaspoon dried chilli flakes
2 tablespoons chopped fresh
   flat-leaf parsley

1 Heat 1 tablespoon of the oil in large non-stick frying pan. Cook fish, flesh-side down, until well browned. Turn fish; cook until browned and just cooked through.
2 Meanwhile, place remaining oil, garlic, vinegar, chilli and parsley in small saucepan; stir over low heat until just warm – do not overheat. Spoon oil mixture over fish. Serve with lemon wedges and steamed courgette and beans, if desired.

preparation time 5 minutes
cooking time 8 minutes
serves 4
per serving 18.2g fat; 1376kJ (329 cal)
tip Sherry vinegar is available in some supermarkets; if unavailable, substitute red or white wine vinegar.

cumin fish cutlets
with coriander chilli sauce

6 firm white fish cutlets (1.2kg)
2 teaspoons cumin seeds

coriander chilli sauce
8 spring onions, chopped coarsely
3 cloves garlic, crushed
3 fresh red thai chillies, deseeded,
    chopped finely
1 tablespoon finely chopped
    coriander root
2 tablespoons brown sugar
2 tablespoons fish sauce
¼ cup (60ml) lime juice

1 Sprinkle one side of each cutlet with seeds. Cook fish on heated oiled barbecue plate, until browned on both sides and just cooked through.
2 Serve fish with coriander chilli sauce and lime, if desired.

coriander chilli sauce Using the 'pulse' button, blend or process onion, garlic, chilli, coriander root and sugar until chopped finely. Add sauce and juice; blend until combined.

preparation time 15 minutes
cooking time 10 minutes
serves 6
per serving 4.3g fat; 915kJ (218 cal)
tip This recipe is best made just before serving.

seared tuna with chilled soba

200g dried soba noodles
¼ cup (60ml) mirin
2 tablespoons kecap manis
1 tablespoon cooking sake
2 teaspoons white sugar
5cm piece fresh ginger (25g), grated
1 clove garlic, crushed
4 tuna steaks (800g)
1 sheet toasted seaweed (yaki-nori),
    sliced thinly
2 spring onions, chopped finely
1 teaspoon sesame oil
2 tablespoons coarsely chopped
    vietnamese mint
2 tablespoons pickled ginger, sliced
    thinly

1 Cook soba in large saucepan of boiling water, uncovered, until just tender; drain. Rinse under cold water; drain. Place in medium bowl, cover; refrigerate until required.
2 Meanwhile, combine mirin, kecap manis, sake, sugar, fresh ginger and garlic in small jug.
3 Cook fish in heated lightly oiled large frying pan, uncovered, until cooked as desired (tuna can become very dry if overcooked; we recommend you sear it over very high heat for about 30 seconds each side). Add mirin mixture to pan; coat fish both sides in mixture. Remove fish from pan; cover to keep warm.
4 Bring mixture in pan to a boil. Reduce heat; simmer, uncovered, 30 seconds. Strain sauce into small jug.
5 Meanwhile, place seaweed, onion, oil, mint and pickled ginger in bowl with soba; toss gently to combine. Divide fish among plates, drizzle with sauce; top with soba. Serve with wasabi, if desired.

preparation time 15 minutes (plus refrigeration time)
cooking time 5 minutes
serves 4
per serving 13.2g fat; 2182kJ (522 cal)

Fleshy, tender leaves like mint (and basil and sage) darken and become limp quickly once they've been chopped so it's a good idea not to handle them until the last possible minute, particularly if they're being used raw. In the picture above, you can see the difference in whole leaves, coarsely chopped then finely chopped mint.

swordfish with thai dressing

4 swordfish steaks (720g)

thai dressing
⅓ cup (80ml) sweet chilli sauce
½ cup (125ml) lime juice
1 tablespoon fish sauce
2 teaspoons finely chopped lemongrass
2 tablespoons chopped fresh coriander
½ cup chopped fresh mint
1 teaspoon grated fresh ginger

1 Cook fish on heated oiled barbecue plate until browned both sides and cooked as desired.
2 Drizzle thai dressing over fish; serve with mixed salad leaves and lemon, if desired.

thai dressing Combine ingredients in screw-top jar; shake well.

preparation time 5 minutes
cooking time 10 minutes
serves 4
per serving 4.7g fat; 918kJ (219 cal)
tip This recipe is best made just before serving.

sumac, salt & pepper fish with mediterranean salad

2 tablespoons sumac
1 teaspoon salt
1 teaspoon cracked black pepper
4 firm white fish fillets (800g)
1 cup (200g) couscous
1 cup (250ml) boiling water
1 tablespoon olive oil
1 lemon, quartered

mediterranean salad
2 medium tomatoes (300g), deseeded, chopped coarsely
2 medium red peppers (400g), chopped coarsely
2 tablespoons pitted black olives, chopped coarsely
2 tablespoons drained baby capers, rinsed
1 cup coarsely chopped fresh flat-leaf parsley

1 Combine sumac, salt and pepper in large bowl, add fish; turn fish to coat in mixture. Cook fish, in batches, in heated lightly oiled large frying pan until cooked as desired.
2 Meanwhile, place mediterranean salad ingredients in medium bowl; toss gently to combine.
3 Combine couscous with the water in large heatproof bowl. Cover; stand about 5 minutes or until water is absorbed, fluffing with fork occasionally. Stir in oil. Divide couscous among plates, top with salad and fish; serve with lemon.

preparation time 20 minutes
cooking time 10 minutes
serves 4
per serving 9.7g fat; 1990kJ (476 cal)
tip You can use any firm white-fleshed fish fillets for this recipe.

thai-flavoured mussels

2kg large black mussels
2 tablespoons water
⅓ cup (80ml) lime juice
2 tablespoons grated palm sugar
2 tablespoons fish sauce
1 fresh long red chilli, chopped finely
2 teaspoons groundnut oil
10cm stick (20g) finely chopped fresh
  lemongrass
1 clove garlic, crushed
4cm piece fresh ginger (20g), grated
2 teaspoons finely chopped coriander
  roots and stems
2 spring onions, sliced thinly
½ cup firmly packed fresh coriander
  leaves
½ cup firmly packed fresh thai basil
  leaves
2 fresh long red chillies, sliced thinly

1 Scrub mussels under cold water; discard beards.
2 Whisk the water, juice, sugar, sauce and chopped chilli in small jug.
3 Heat oil in large saucepan; cook lemongrass, garlic, ginger and coriander roots and stems, stirring, until fragrant. Stir in lime mixture; bring to a boil. Add mussels; return to a boil. Reduce heat; simmer, covered, about 5 minutes or until mussels open (discard any that do not).
4 Divide mussels and cooking liquid among plates; sprinkle with onion, coriander leaves, basil and sliced chilli.

preparation time 30 minutes
cooking time 10 minutes
serves 4
per serving 4.2g fat; 594kJ (142 cal)
tip When removing the leaves from a bunch of coriander, remove some of the stems and roots for this recipe.

Always press the trimmed basil and coriander leaves firmly into a measuring cup so that the proportion of the herb to the other ingredients is correct.

thai pork salad
with kaffir lime dressing

600g pork fillets
2 tablespoons grated palm sugar
1 tablespoon finely grated lime rind
2 teaspoons groundnut oil
350g watercress, trimmed
1 cup loosely packed fresh thai basil
  leaves
½ cup loosely packed fresh coriander
  leaves
½ cup loosely packed fresh mint leaves
1½ cups (120g) beansprouts
1 medium green pepper (200g), sliced
  thinly

kaffir lime dressing
2 cloves garlic, crushed
3 shallots (75g), sliced thinly
1 fresh small red thai chilli, sliced thinly
3 fresh kaffir lime leaves, sliced thinly
¼ cup (60ml) lime juice
⅓ cup (80ml) fish sauce
2 teaspoons grated palm sugar

1 Cut pork fillets in half horizontally. Combine sugar, rind and oil in large bowl, add pork; toss pork to coat in mixture. Cook pork, in batches, in heated lightly oiled large frying pan, over medium heat, about 15 minutes or until cooked as desired. Cover pork; stand 5 minutes, then slice thinly.
2 Meanwhile, make kaffir lime dressing.
3 Place pork in large bowl with remaining ingredients, add dressing; toss gently to combine.

kaffir lime dressing Place all dressing ingredients in screw-top jar; shake well.

preparation time 15 minutes
cooking time 15 minutes
serves 4
per serving 6.4g fat; 1104kJ (264 cal)

Tossing in a few herbs can really give a salad a new slant.
And if you add a few spices to the dressing, then even
a plain green salad can be a new taste experience!

chicken salads...

chicken & coriander

2½ cups (425g) chopped cooked chicken
500g spinach, trimmed
100g watercress
1 medium (200g) red pepper, chopped
4 spring onions, chopped
250g cherry tomatoes, halved
½ cucumber, sliced
¼ cup chopped fresh coriander leaves

chilli dressing
⅓ cup (80ml) vegetable oil
1 tablespoon soy sauce
2 tablespoons sweet chilli sauce
½ teaspoon sesame oil
¼ cup (60ml) white vinegar
½ teaspoon sugar

1 Combine chicken with torn spinach leaves
and remaining ingredients in large bowl.
2 Just before serving, add warm dressing;
toss gently.

chilli dressing Combine ingredients in small
pan; whisk over heat until warm. Do not boil.

preparation time 30 minutes • **serves** 4
tip You will need 1 large cooked chicken for
this recipe.

chicken, peach & mint

80g cooked chicken, shredded
1½ cups shredded chinese cabbage
¼ cup shredded fresh mint leaves
1 small peach, cut into wedges

lime dressing
2 tablespoons lime juice
1 teaspoon olive oil.

1 Combine chicken, chinese cabbage, mint
leaves and peach in a small bowl.
2 Toss dressing with salad.

lime dressing Combine lime juice and olive oil
in a small bowl.

preparation time 10 minutes • **serves** 1

chicken salad with ginger soy dressing

1 tablespoon groundnut oil
4 (680g) chicken breast fillets
1 small (400g) chinese cabbage, shredded
4 spring onions, chopped
4 sticks celery, sliced
50g watercress

ginger soy dressing
¼ cup (60ml) groundnut oil
2 tablespoons soy sauce
1 teaspoon sesame oil
1 teaspoon grated fresh ginger
1 clove garlic, crushed
½ teaspoon sugar
2 tablespoons lime juice

1 Heat oil in frying pan; cook chicken until browned both sides and cooked through; slice thinly.
2 Combine chicken, cabbage, onion and celery in bowl, top with watercress; drizzle with soy dressing.

ginger soy dressing Combine ingredients in screw-topped jar; shake well.

preparation time 30 minutes • **serves** 4

mexican chicken & bean

2 cups (340g) chopped cooked chicken
1 cos lettuce, torn roughly
250g cherry tomatoes, halved
250g yellow teardrop tomatoes, halved
1 medium (200g) red pepper, sliced
1 medium (200g) green pepper, sliced
1 medium (170g) red onion, sliced
300g can corn kernels, rinsed, drained
2 x 300g cans kidney beans, rinsed, drained
1 medium (250g) avocado
⅓ cup (80ml) soured cream

spicy dressing
⅓ cup (80ml) olive oil
1 tablespoon lime juice
1 tablespoon sweet chilli sauce
1 small fresh red chilli, deseeded, chopped
1 teaspoon hot paprika

1 Combine chicken with lettuce, tomatoes, pepper, onion, corn, beans and dressing.
2 Scoop flesh from the avocado; mash well with fork. Serve salad topped with mashed avocado and soured cream.

spicy dressing Combine dressing ingredients in screw-topped jar; shake well.

preparation time 40 minutes • **serves** 4

prawn salads...

thai-style prawn & mango

20 (1kg) large cooked prawns
3 large (1.8kg) mangoes, chopped
1 large (300g) red onion, sliced
⅓ cup firmly packed fresh coriander leaves
500g cherry tomatoes, halved
660g yellow teardrop tomatoes, halved
2 tablespoons sesame seeds, toasted
2 large (640g) avocados, sliced

thai dressing
1 clove garlic, crushed
1 small fresh red chilli, deseeded, quartered
1 medium (190g) tomato, peeled, quartered
2 tablespoons lime juice
1 teaspoon sugar
2 teaspoons rice vinegar
2 teaspoons chopped fresh coriander leaves
¼ cup (60ml) groundnut oil
1 teaspoon grated fresh ginger

1 Shell and devein prawns, leaving tails intact.
Combine prawns with remaining ingredients in
large bowl; add dressing, toss gently.
2 Serve on watercress, if desired.

thai dressing Blend all ingredients until
smooth.

preparation time 45 minutes • serves 4

prawn & cabbage salad with minty dressing

20 (1kg) large cooked prawns
3 cups (240g) shredded cabbage
1 cup (80g) shredded red cabbage
1 stick celery, sliced
½ (130g) cucumber, sliced
1 medium (200g) red pepper, sliced

minty dressing
¼ cup (60ml) olive oil
¼ cup (60ml) orange juice
2 tablespoons lemon juice
1½ teaspoons fish sauce
¼ cup chopped fresh mint leaves
2 teaspoons sugar

1 Shell and devein prawns, leaving tails intact.
Combine ingredients in large bowl; pour over
dressing, mix gently.

minty dressing Combine ingredients in
screw-topped jar; shake well.

preparation time 50 minutes • serves 4

tuna salads...

tuna salad with beans

1 medium (200g) red pepper, quartered
9 (360g) tiny new potatoes, halved
300g green beans
2 medium (380g) tomatoes, chopped
1 small round lettuce
425g can tuna, drained and flaked
2 hard-boiled eggs, quartered
¼ cup (40g) pitted black olives

herb dressing
½ cup (125ml) olive oil
¼ cup (60ml) balsamic vinegar
1 tablespoon dijon mustard
¼ cup shredded fresh basil leaves
1 tablespoon chopped fresh thyme

1 Roast pepper under grill, skin-side up, until skin blisters. Cover with cling film for 5 minutes; peel away skin. Cut flesh into thin strips.
2 Cook potatoes until tender; drain. Combine warm potatoes with one-third of the dressing.
3 Cook beans until tender, rinse in cold water, drain. Combine tomatoes with one-third of the dressing. Arrange lettuce on plate, top with tuna, eggs and vegetables; drizzle with dressing.

herb dressing Combine ingredients in screw-topped jar; shake well.

preparation time 40 minutes • serves 4

tuna & spinach salad with dill

125g can tuna in spring water, drained, sliced
2 cups baby spinach leaves, trimmed
1½ teaspoons baby capers, rinsed, drained
⅓ cup cherry tomatoes, halved
3 teaspoons fresh dill sprigs

lemon dressing
1 tablespoon lemon juice
1 teaspoon olive oil

1 Combine tuna spinach leaves, capers, tomatoes and dill sprigs in a small bowl.
2 Toss dressing with salad.

lemon dressing Combine lemon juice and olive oil in a small bowl.

preparation time 5 minutes • serves 1

noodle salads...

beef noodle

500g beef fillet steak
300g hokkien noodles
2 teaspoons vegetable oil
500g baby pak choy, chopped
500g choy sum, chopped
1 bunch (500g) chinese broccoli, chopped
1 small (400g) chinese cabbage, shredded
1 cup (80g) beansprouts

chilli lemongrass dressing
2 tablespoons chopped lemongrass
2 small fresh red chillies, deseeded, sliced
2 tablespoons each soy sauce and lime juice
1 tablespoon grated fresh ginger
1 teaspoon sugar

1 Marinate the beef in a third of the dressing for 10 minutes. Grill beef until browned and cooked through. Cover, stand 5 minutes; slice.
2 Soak noodles in boiling water for 5 minutes; drain. Heat oil in wok; quickly stir-fry pak choy, choy sum and broccoli until just wilted.
3 Gently combine beef with vegetables, noodles, cabbage, sprouts and rest of dressing.

chilli lemongrass dressing Combine ingredients in screw-topped jar; shake well.

preparation time 40 minutes • **serves** 4

scallop & tomato noodle

250g dried rice noodles
500g white scallops
1 tablespoon sweet chilli sauce
1 tablespoon lime juice
250g asparagus, trimmed, chopped
330g yellow teardrop tomatoes, halved
⅓ cup (25g) flaked almonds, toasted

lime dressing
½ cup (125ml) groundnut oil
1 teaspoon brown sugar
2 tablespoons chopped fresh coriander leaves
1 tablespoon chopped fresh mint leaves
2 small fresh red chillies, deseeded, quartered
¼ cup (60ml) lime juice

1 Place noodles in large heatproof bowl, cover with boiling water, stand only until just tender; drain. Rinse under cold water; drain.
2 Grill scallops, in batches, until changed in colour, brushing occasionally with combined chilli sauce and juice. Steam asparagus until just tender; rinse under cold water, drain.
3 Gently toss noodles, scallops, asparagus and tomatoes with dressing; sprinkle with nuts.

lime dressing Blend ingredients until smooth.

preparation time 40 minutes • **serves** 4

vegetarian salads...

chickpea salad

½ cup canned chickpeas, rinsed, drained
½ cucumber, coarsely chopped
½ small red onion, thinly sliced
¼ cup pitted black olives
⅓ cup fresh flat-leaf parsley leaves
¼ cup coarsely chopped yellow pepper
1 small plum tomato, deseeded and cut into
   wedges
2 tablespoons prepared low-fat tzatziki

lemon & cumin dressing
1 tablespoon lemon juice
1 teaspoon olive oil
¼ teaspoon finely chopped lemon rind
¼ teaspoon ground cumin

1   Combine chickpeas, chopped cucumber,
onion, olives, flat-leaf parsley leaves, pepper
and tomato wedges in a small bowl.
2   Toss dressing with the salad and serve
topped with tzatziki.

lemon & cumin dressing Combine all the
ingredients in a small bowl.

preparation time 15 minutes • **serves** 1

butterbean, tomato & rocket

9 large (800g) plum tomatoes
2 x 300g cans butterbeans, rinsed, drained
1 medium (170g) red onion, sliced thinly
120g rocket, trimmed, chopped roughly
2 tablespoons slivered almonds, toasted

spicy herb dressing
2 cloves garlic, crushed
¾ cup (180ml) olive oil
½ cup (125ml) lemon juice
¼ cup chopped fresh parsley
1½ tablespoons sugar
3 teaspoons sweet paprika
1 teaspoon chilli powder

1   Halve tomatoes lengthways, remove seeds,
slice tomato thinly.
2   Combine tomato, beans, onion, rocket and
dressing in large bowl; mix well. Serve topped
with nuts.

spicy herb dressing Combine ingredients in
screw-topped jar; shake well.

preparation time 30 minutes • **serves** 4

beef salads...

satay beef salad

500g piece beef eye-fillet
2 medium (240g) carrots
3 cups (240g) beansprouts
100g mustard and cress
1 medium (170g) red onion, sliced
¼ cup loosely packed fresh coriander leaves
⅓ cup (50g) unsalted roast peanuts, chopped

satay sauce
2 tablespoons brown sugar
2 tablespoons chopped fresh coriander leaves
¼ cup (60ml) sweet chilli sauce
½ cup (130g) smooth peanut butter
2 cloves garlic, crushed
½ cup (125ml) coconut milk
½ cup (125ml) water

1 Grill beef, uncovered, about 20 minutes or until browned and cooked as desired. Cover and stand 10 minutes before slicing thinly.
2 Cut carrots lengthways into long thin strips, using a vegetable peeler. Combine carrot, beef, sprouts, cress and onion in bowl, drizzle with sauce; sprinkle with coriander and peanuts.

satay sauce Combine ingredients in small pan; simmer, stirring, until sauce thickens; cool slightly.

preparation time 45 minutes • serves 4

sesame beef salad

500g piece beef eye-fillet
1 teaspoon grated fresh ginger
1 clove garlic, crushed
¼ cup (60ml) each soy sauce and sweet sherry
2 tablespoons sesame oil
250g asparagus, trimmed, chopped
150g mangetout
250g dried wheat noodles
1 teaspoon dijon mustard
2 teaspoons honey
1 tablespoon white wine vinegar
2 tablespoons olive oil
1 tablespoon sesame seeds, toasted

1 Combine beef with ginger, garlic, sauce, sherry and sesame oil. Cover; chill 10 minutes.
2 Steam asparagus and mangetout, separately, until just tender; drain. Rinse, drain well.
3 Cook noodles in boiling water until just tender; drain. Rinse under cold water; drain.
4 Drain beef, reserving marinade. Cook beef in oiled frying pan until brown and cooked as desired. Remove from pan; cover, stand 10 minutes, slice thinly. Add marinade to pan; simmer, uncovered, 2 minutes until it thickens.
5 Combine with mustard, honey, vinegar and olive oil. Toss beef, asparagus, mangetout and noodles with dressing and sesame seeds.

preparation time 50 minutes • serves 4

lamb salads...

lamb, bean & parmesan

500g lamb eye of loin
200g green beans, chopped
200g butterbeans, chopped
350g watercress, trimmed
1 medium (170g) red onion, sliced

parmesan dressing
½ cup (40g) finely grated parmesan cheese
½ cup chopped fresh flat-leaf parsley
½ cup (125ml) olive oil
½ cup (125ml) white wine vinegar
2 cloves garlic, crushed

1 Griddle-fry (or grill or barbecue) lamb, until browned all over and cooked as desired. Remove from pan, cover; stand 5 minutes. Slice lamb thinly.
2 Boil, steam or microwave both beans until just tender, rinse under cold water; drain.
3 Combine lamb with beans, watercress and onion in large bowl; drizzle with the parmesan dressing.

parmesan dressing Blend or process ingredients until smooth and creamy.

preparation time 35 minutes • serves 4

lamb, tomato & mozzarella salad with basil

2 (800g) lamb mini roasts
2 medium (380g) tomatoes, sliced
¼ cup firmly packed fresh basil leaves
250g mozzarella, sliced
½ cup (125ml) light olive oil
2 tablespoons red wine vinegar
2 teaspoons dijon mustard
1 teaspoon sugar
1 clove garlic, crushed
2 teaspoons olive paste

1 Place lamb in large oiled baking dish; bake, uncovered, in moderate oven for about 25 minutes or until cooked as desired. Cover lamb, stand 5 minutes; slice thinly.
2 Layer lamb, tomato, basil and mozzarella on platter; drizzle with combined remaining ingredients.

preparation time 45 minutes • serves 4

pork salads...

gingered pork salad

500g lean pork strips
3 teaspoons grated fresh ginger
3 teaspoons sesame oil
1 tablespoon soy sauce
1 tablespoon cider vinegar
3 (450g) baby pak choy
250g mangetout
1 tablespoon finely grated lime rind
¼ cup (60ml) lime juice
2 tablespoons chopped fresh coriander leaves
2½ cups (200g) beansprouts

1 Combine pork with ginger, half of the oil, half of the sauce and half of the vinegar in bowl, cover; refrigerate 10 minutes.
2 Discard stems from pak choy. Cover pak choy and mangetout with boiling water; stand 2 minutes. Drain, rinse under cold water; drain.
3 Cook undrained pork, in batches, in heated non-stick frying pan, stirring, until tender.
4 Combine remaining oil, sauce and vinegar with rind, juice and coriander in screw-topped jar; shake well. Toss ingredients together in large bowl. Top with chives and chopped chilli, if desired.

preparation time 45 minutes • **serves** 4

ham & crispy potato

25 (1kg) tiny new potatoes, halved
2 teaspoons olive oil
1 tablespoon lemon pepper seasoning
180g green beans
400g lean leg ham, thinly sliced
100g mixed baby salad leaves
1 large (320g) avocado, chopped

orange mustard dressing
½ cup (125ml) orange juice
2 tablespoons lemon juice
2 teaspoons dijon mustard
1 teaspoon balsamic vinegar
1 clove garlic, crushed
1 teaspoon caster sugar

1 Combine potatoes, oil and seasoning in large non-stick baking dish; bake, uncovered, in very hot oven about 25 minutes or until browned and tender. Cook beans until just tender, rinse under cold water; drain.
2 Combine potatoes, beans, ham, salad leaves and avocado in bowl. Drizzle dressing over salad just before serving.

orange mustard dressing Combine ingredients in screw-topped jar; shake well.

preparation time 45 minutes • **serves** 4

pasta salads...

cabanossi & basil pasta salad

300g penne pasta
2 cabanossi sausages, sliced
1 medium (200g) red pepper, sliced
2 medium (240g) courgettes, sliced
4 spring onions, sliced
1 tablespoon chopped fresh basil leaves
2 tablespoons finely grated parmesan cheese
½ cup (125ml) bottled Italian salad dressing

1 Cook pasta in large saucepan of boiling water, uncovered, until just tender; drain.
2 Combine pasta with remaining ingredients in large bowl; toss together gently.

preparation time 25 minutes • **serves 4**

pasta salad with pesto dressing

500g bow-tie pasta
200g mozzarella
100g sliced hot salami, cut into strips
1 cup (150g) drained sliced sun-dried tomatoes in oil
½ cup (80g) black olives, deseeded, chopped
¼ cup chopped fresh chives
2 tablespoons pine nuts, toasted

pesto dressing
⅓ cup (80ml) olive oil
1 tablespoon lime juice
½ cup loosely packed fresh basil leaves
1 tablespoon grated parmesan
1 teaspoon sugar

1 Cook pasta in large saucepan of boiling water, uncovered, until just tender; drain. Rinse under cold water; drain well.
2 Slice cheese; cut into strips. Combine pasta with cheese, salami, tomatoes, olives and chives. Just before serving, toss pesto dressing through pasta mixture; sprinkle with nuts.

pesto dressing Blend ingredients until smooth.

preparation time 40 minutes • **serves 4**

butternut squash & split pea tagine

1 cup (200g) green split peas
1 tablespoon olive oil
1 medium brown onion (150g),
    chopped finely
2 cloves garlic, crushed
2 teaspoons ground coriander
2 teaspoons ground cumin
2 teaspoons ground ginger
1 teaspoon sweet paprika
1 teaspoon ground allspice
1kg butternut squash, peeled and
    diced into 3cm pieces
425g can crushed tomatoes
1 cup (250ml) water
1 cup (250ml) vegetable stock
2 tablespoons honey
200g green beans, trimmed, chopped
    coarsely
¼ cup coarsely chopped fresh
    coriander

1 Cook split peas in medium saucepan of boiling water, uncovered, until just tender; drain. Rinse under cold water; drain.
2 Meanwhile, heat oil in large saucepan; cook onion, stirring, until softened. Add garlic and spices; cook, stirring, about 2 minutes or until fragrant. Add squash; stir squash to coat in spice mixture.
3 Stir in undrained tomatoes, the water and stock; bring to a boil. Reduce heat; simmer, uncovered, about 20 minutes or until squash is just tender.
Stir in honey then beans and split peas, reduce heat; simmer, uncovered, about 10 minutes or until beans are just tender. Remove from heat; stir in coriander. Serve with steamed couscous, if desired.

preparation time 15 minutes
cooking time 40 minutes
serves 4
per serving 7g fat; 1484kJ (355 cal)

Vegetables need not be boring — here are some ideas for rich, flavoursome meals and side dishes that are far from bland and uninteresting!

ciabatta with olive & herb paste

1 loaf ciabatta
2 tablespoons olive oil

olive and herb paste
250g pitted green olives
½ small white onion (40g), chopped
freshly ground black pepper
1 clove garlic, crushed
¼ cup (60ml) extra virgin olive oil
1 tablespoon coarsely chopped
   fresh flat-leaf parsley
1 teaspoon coarsely chopped
   fresh oregano
1 teaspoon lime juice

1 Preheat oven to moderately hot.
2 Cut bread into 1cm slices. Place bread in single layer on baking trays; brush with oil. Bake in moderately hot oven about 5 minutes on each side or until browned lightly and crisp; cool.
3 Serve ciabatta with olive and herb paste.

olive and herb paste Process olives, onion, pepper and garlic into a coarse paste. Gradually add oil while motor is operating; stir in herbs and juice.

preparation time 20 minutes
cooking time 10 minutes (plus cooling time)
serves 6
per serving 19.4g fat; 1845kJ (441 cal)
tip Recipe can be prepared a day ahead and refrigerated, covered separately.

grilled feta with chilli

300g feta cheese, halved
2 tablespoons olive oil
1 teaspoon chilli flakes
1 teaspoon dried oregano leaves

1 Line a baking tray with large sheet of foil. Place feta on top of foil.
2 Combine oil, chilli and oregano in small bowl; drizzle over cheese. Grill about 5 minutes or until browned lightly. Stand 5 minutes; slice thickly.

preparation time 5 minutes
cooking time 5 minutes
serves 6
per serving 17.8g fat; 817kJ (195 cal)

baked ricotta with roasted pepper salad

200g low-fat ricotta cheese
2 tablespoons finely grated parmesan cheese
1 egg, beaten lightly
1 teaspoon coarsely chopped fresh sage leaves
3 fresh bay leaves, chopped coarsely
2 medium red peppers (400g)
2 medium yellow peppers (400g)
250g mixed baby salad leaves
¼ cup (60ml) balsamic vinegar
1 tablespoon olive oil
1 tablespoon honey

1 Preheat oven to moderately low.
2 Oil eight holes of a 12-hole ⅓-cup (80ml) non-stick muffin tray. Combine cheeses and egg in small bowl. Divide ricotta mixture among prepared tray holes; sprinkle with combined herbs.
3 Place muffin tray in large baking dish; add enough boiling water to come halfway up side of tray. Bake ricotta, uncovered, in moderately low oven about 30 minutes or until set. Stand 10 minutes before turning out ricotta.
4 Meanwhile, quarter peppers; remove and discard seeds and membranes. Roast under grill or in very hot oven, skin-side up, until skin blisters and blackens. Cover pepper pieces with plastic or paper 5 minutes. Peel away and discard skin; slice pepper flesh thickly.
5 Place pepper and salad leaves in large bowl with combined remaining ingredients. Divide salad among serving plates; top each with a baked ricotta.

preparation time 15 minutes
cooking time 30 minutes
(plus standing time)
serves 8
per serving 5.8g fat; 430kJ (103 cal)
tip Dried bay leaves and ¼ teaspoon crumbled dried sage can be substituted for the fresh varieties.

chickpea & corn enchiladas

1 tablespoon olive oil

1 small brown onion (80g), chopped
  coarsely

1 clove garlic, crushed

1 teaspoon sweet paprika

½ teaspoon ground chilli powder

1 teaspoon ground cumin

400g can tomato purée

300g can chickpeas, rinsed, drained

1 tablespoon chopped fresh coriander

8 corn tortillas

1 small red onion (100g), chopped
  coarsely

1 medium tomato (190g), chopped
  coarsely

1 small avocado (200g), chopped
  coarsely

½ cup (60g) coarsely grated cheddar
  cheese

½ cup finely shredded iceberg lettuce

1 Heat oil in medium saucepan; cook onion and garlic, stirring, until onion softens. Add spices; cook, stirring, 2 minutes. Add tomato purée; bring to a boil. Reduce heat; simmer, stirring occasionally, 5 minutes. Add chickpeas and coriander; cook, stirring, until hot.

2 Soften tortillas in microwave oven on HIGH (100%) for 30 seconds.

3 Divide chickpea mixture and remaining ingredients among tortillas; fold enchiladas to enclose filling.

preparation time 15 minutes
cooking time 10 minutes
serves 4
per serving 21.2g fat; 1972kJ
(472 cal)

tips We used 16cm-round corn tortillas, which come vacuum-packed. Unused tortillas can be frozen in freezer bags for up to 3 weeks. You can also soften tortillas by wrapping them in foil and heating them in a moderate oven about 5 minutes or until hot.

koshari

Various combinations of rice and lentils are eaten throughout the Middle East and India, with perhaps the two most well-known versions being Lebanese mujadara and Indian kitcheree. Our Egyptian take on this homely dish, however, adds delicious 'oomph' to the rice-lentil theme with its fragrantly spicy caramelised onion and piquant chilli sauce.

2 cups (400g) brown lentils
¾ cup (150g) white long-grain rice
1 cup coarsely chopped fresh
    flat-leaf parsley

caramelised onion
2 tablespoons olive oil
5 large brown onions (1kg), sliced thinly
1½ teaspoons ground allspice
1 teaspoon ground coriander
2 teaspoons white sugar

tomato chilli sauce
2 teaspoons olive oil
3 cloves garlic, crushed
½ teaspoon ground cumin
½ teaspoon dried chilli flakes
⅓ cup (80ml) white vinegar
415ml can tomato juice

1 Make caramelised onion. Make tomato chilli sauce.
2 Meanwhile, cook lentils in medium saucepan of boiling water, uncovered, until just tender; drain.
3 Cook rice in medium saucepan of boiling water, uncovered, until just tender; drain.
4 Remove half of the caramelised onion from pan, reserve. Add lentils and rice to pan, stirring, until heated through. Remove from heat; stir in half of the parsley.
5 Divide koshari among bowls; top with reserved caramelised onion, remaining parsley and tomato chilli sauce.

caramelised onion Heat oil in large frying pan; cook onion, allspice and coriander, stirring, until onion softens. Add sugar; cook, uncovered, stirring occasionally, about 30 minutes or until onion caramelises.

tomato chilli sauce Heat oil in small saucepan; cook garlic, cumin and chilli, stirring, until fragrant. Add vinegar and juice; bring to a boil. Boil, uncovered, 2 minutes.

preparation time 15 minutes
cooking time 45 minutes
serves 4
per serving 13.9g fat; 2416kJ (578 cal)

pak choy steamed with chilli oil

4 baby pak choy (600g)
1 tablespoon groundnut oil
2 cloves garlic, crushed
2 tablespoons light soy sauce
1½ teaspoons hot chilli sauce
2 spring onions, sliced thinly
¼ cup fresh coriander leaves
1 fresh red thai chilli, deseeded,
    sliced thinly

1 Halve pak choy lengthways; place, cut-side up, in bamboo steamer. Drizzle pak choy with combined oil, garlic and sauces.
2 Steam pak choy, covered, over wok or large saucepan of simmering water about 5 minutes or until just tender. Serve pak choy sprinkled with onion, coriander and chilli.

preparation time 5 minutes
cooking time 5 minutes
serves 4
per serving 5g fat; 273kJ (65 cal)

spicy potato

6 medium potatoes (1.2kg), chopped
¼ cup (60ml) groundnut oil
1 teaspoon black mustard seeds
1 teaspoon cumin seeds
1 teaspoon ground cumin
½ teaspoon sweet paprika
1½ teaspoons ground turmeric
¼ teaspoon chilli flakes
1 clove garlic, crushed
2 tablespoons lemon juice
¼ cup chopped fresh coriander

preparation time 10 minutes
cooking time 30 minutes (plus cooling time)
serves 6
per serving 10.2g fat; 960kJ (230 cal)

1 Preheat oven to hot. Boil, steam or microwave potato until just tender; rinse under cold running water. Drain potato; cool.
2 Combine potato, oil, seeds, spices, garlic and juice in baking dish. Cook in hot oven about 20 minutes or until potato is brown. Top with coriander to serve.

chilli cauliflower with pine nuts

1 small cauliflower (1kg)
2 tablespoons extra virgin olive oil
2 cloves garlic, crushed
2 tablespoons pine nuts
2 teaspoons chopped dried chilli
2 tablespoons chopped fresh flat-leaf
  parsley

1 Separate cauliflower into pieces. Boil, steam or microwave until almost tender. Drain; pat dry.
2 Heat oil in medium frying pan; cook garlic, pine nuts and chilli, stirring, over low heat until fragrant and nuts are browned lightly.
3 Add cauliflower; cook, stirring, until well coated with oil mixture. Add parsley; stir until combined.

preparation time 10 minutes
cooking time 10 minutes
serves 8
per serving 7.5g fat; 385kJ (92 cal)
tip This recipe is best made just before serving.

spiced stone-fruit strudel

2 medium peaches (300g), quartered,
sliced thinly
2 medium nectarines (340g), quartered,
sliced thinly
2 tablespoons brown sugar
½ cup (80g) sultanas
1½ teaspoons ground cinnamon
½ teaspoon ground nutmeg
⅓ cup (25g) fresh breadcrumbs
6 sheets filo pastry
20g butter, melted
2 tablespoons milk
2 teaspoons icing sugar

1   Combine peach, nectarine, brown sugar, sultanas, spices and breadcrumbs in medium bowl.
2   Preheat oven to moderately hot. Grease baking tray and line with baking parchment.
3   Stack filo sheets, brushing all sheets lightly with half of the combined butter and milk. Cut filo stack in half widthways; cover one stack with baking parchment, then with a damp tea towel, to prevent drying out.
4   Place half of the fruit mixture along centre of uncovered filo stack; roll from one side to enclose filling, sealing ends of roll with a little of the remaining butter mixture. Place strudel, seam-side down, on prepared tray; brush all over with a little of the remaining butter mixture. Repeat process with remaining filo stack, fruit mixture and butter mixture.
5   Bake strudels, uncovered, in moderately hot oven about 25 minutes or until browned lightly. Cut each strudel in half widthways; divide among plates, dust with sifted icing sugar.

preparation time 20 minutes
cooking time 25 minutes
serves 4
per serving 5.5g fat; 1191kJ (285 cal)
tip You can use canned peaches and nectarines if fresh ones aren't available.

Enjoy scrumptious spicy treats such as meringues with banana and caramel sauce or figs with spiced yogurt as a divinely decadent dessert, or feast on some yummy rock cakes or ginger muffins with your afternoon tea.

banana muffins
with crunchy topping

1¾ cups (280g) wholemeal self-raising flour
¾ cup (165g) firmly packed brown sugar
1 cup mashed banana (you will need approximately two large (460g) overripe bananas)
1 egg, beaten lightly
1 cup (250ml) buttermilk
¼ cup (60ml) vegetable oil

crunchy oat topping
1 cup (90g) rolled oats
½ teaspoon ground nutmeg
2 tablespoons honey

1 Preheat oven to moderately hot. Lightly grease 12-hole (⅓-cup/80ml) muffin tray.
2 Make crunchy oat topping.
3 Sift flour and sugar into large bowl; stir in banana, egg, buttermilk and oil. Divide mixture among prepared holes of muffin tray; sprinkle with topping.
4 Bake, uncovered, in moderately hot oven about 20 minutes. Stand muffins in tray 5 minutes; turn onto wire rack to cool.

crunchy oat topping Blend or process oats until coarsely chopped. Combine oats, nutmeg and honey in small bowl.

preparation time 20 minutes
cooking time 20 minutes
makes 12
per muffin 6.6g fat; 1041kJ (249 cal)

ginger muffins & stewed pear

3 teaspoons ground ginger

⅔ cup (100g) coarsely chopped dried apricots

½ cup (95g) coarsely chopped dried figs

1⅓ cups (95g) All-Bran breakfast cereal

1½ cups (375ml) skimmed milk

1¼ cups (275g) firmly packed brown sugar

⅓ cup (115g) golden syrup

1¼ cups (185g) self-raising flour

¼ cup (35g) toasted pecans, chopped coarsely

3 medium pears (690g), peeled, cut into 8 wedges each

1 cup (250ml) water

1 tablespoon icing sugar

1 Combine ginger, apricot, fig, cereal, milk, brown sugar and half of the golden syrup in large bowl; mix well. Cover; refrigerate overnight.

2 Preheat oven to moderately hot. Lightly grease six-hole (¾-cup/180ml) large muffin tray.

3 Stir flour and nuts into apricot mixture. Spoon mixture into prepared muffin tray; bake, uncovered, in moderately hot oven about 30 minutes. Stand muffins in tray 5 minutes before turning onto wire rack.

4 Meanwhile, combine pear, remaining golden syrup and the water in large frying pan; simmer, covered, about 15 minutes or until pears are soft. Dust muffins with sifted icing sugar; serve with stewed pear.

preparation time 25 minutes (plus refrigeration time)
cooking time 30 minutes
makes 6
per muffin 5.7g fat; 2383kJ (570 cal)
tip Make the batter for these muffins the night before you want to bake and serve them.

cranberry, apricot & currant rock cakes

2 cups (300g) self-raising flour
¼ teaspoon ground cinnamon
90g cold butter, chopped
⅓ cup (75g) caster sugar
½ cup (75g) currants
½ cup (75g) dried apricots, chopped
   coarsely
½ cup (75g) dried cranberries
1 egg, beaten lightly
½ cup (125ml) milk, approximately
1 tablespoon raw cane sugar

1 Preheat oven to moderately hot. Lightly grease two baking trays.
2 Combine flour and cinnamon in large bowl; rub in butter. Stir in caster sugar, dried fruit, egg and enough milk to give a moist but still firm consistency.
3 Drop rounded tablespoons of mixture about 5cm apart on prepared trays; sprinkle with raw sugar. Bake, uncovered, in moderately hot oven about 15 minutes or until browned lightly. Loosen cakes; cool on trays.

preparation time 15 minutes
cooking time 15 minutes
makes 20
per cake 4.2g fat; 564kJ (135 cal)

date & apple muesli slices

2 medium apples (300g), grated
  coarsely
2 tablespoons lemon juice
¼ cup (60ml) water
50g butter
2 cups (340g) stoned dates
2 cups (220g) natural muesli
1 cup (220g) firmly packed brown sugar
1 cup (150g) plain flour
1 teaspoon ground cinnamon
½ teaspoon mixed spice

1 Preheat oven to moderate. Lightly grease a
25cm x 30cm swiss roll tin.
2 Combine apple, juice, the water, butter and dates
in medium saucepan; bring to a boil. Reduce heat;
simmer, covered, about 5 minutes or until apple is soft.
Uncover; cook, stirring occasionally, about 5 minutes
or until mixture thickens to a paste-like consistency.
3 Meanwhile, place muesli in large frying pan; stir
over low heat about 5 minutes or until browned
lightly. Combine muesli in large bowl with sugar, flour,
cinnamon and mixed spice. Stir in date mixture.
4 Spread slice mixture into prepared tin; bake,
uncovered, in moderate oven about 20 minutes or
until firm. Cool in tin before cutting.

preparation time 15 minutes
cooking time 35 minutes
makes 32
per slice 1.6g fat; 326kJ (79 cal)

107

oaty apple pikelets

2 cups (500ml) skimmed milk
1 cup (120g) oat bran
½ cup (75g) plain flour
2 tablespoons brown sugar
½ teaspoon mixed spice
2 eggs
1 large apple (200g), peeled, cored,
   chopped finely
1 tablespoon lemon juice
½ cup (175g) honey
½ cup (100g) low-fat ricotta

1 Blend or process milk, bran, flour, sugar, spice and eggs until smooth; pour into large jug. Stir in apple and juice, cover; refrigerate 30 minutes (mixture will separate during refrigeration).

2 Heat lightly oiled large frying pan. Stir mixture to combine; using ¼-cup batter for each pikelet (mixture will be runny), cook two pikelets at a time, uncovered, until bubbles appear on the surface. Turn; cook until browned lightly. Remove pikelets from pan; cover to keep warm. Repeat with remaining batter to make 12 pikelets.

3 Divide pikelets among plates; drizzle with honey and top with ricotta.

preparation time 10 minutes (plus refrigeration time)
cooking time 15 minutes
serves 4
per serving 7.3g fat; 1973kJ (472 cal)

chocolate rum & raisin loaf

¾ cup (125g) raisins, chopped finely
¼ cup (60ml) dark rum
½ cup (110g) caster sugar
1 egg
1 teaspoon vanilla extract
2 tablespoons golden syrup
80g butter, melted
¾ cup (180ml) buttermilk
1 cup (150g) self-raising flour
2 tablespoons cocoa powder
½ teaspoon ground cinnamon
¼ teaspoon ground nutmeg
⅓ cup (65g) dark chocolate chips

1 Preheat oven to moderate. Lightly grease a
14cm x 21cm loaf tin; line base and two long sides
with baking parchment, extending paper 5cm above
edges of tin.
2 Combine raisins and rum in small bowl; stand,
covered, 2 hours.
3 Beat sugar, egg, extract and syrup in small bowl
with electric mixer until thick and creamy.
4 Transfer mixture to medium bowl; stir in butter,
buttermilk and sifted flour, cocoa, cinnamon and
nutmeg.
Stir in undrained raisin mixture and chocolate chips.
5 Spread mixture into prepared tin; bake, uncovered,
in moderate oven about 45 minutes. Stand 10
minutes; turn onto wire rack to cool.

preparation time 30 minutes (plus standing time)
cooking time 45 minutes
serves 12
per serving 7.7g fat; 932kJ (223 cal)

brown-sugar meringues with banana & caramel sauce

3 egg whites
¾ cup (165g) firmly packed dark brown sugar
3 teaspoons cornflour
3 teaspoons white vinegar
1 teaspoon vanilla extract
10g butter
⅓ cup (80ml) single cream
¼ cup (55g) firmly packed dark brown sugar, extra
½ teaspoon ground nutmeg
½ teaspoon ground ginger
2 medium bananas (400g), sliced thinly

1 Preheat oven to very low.
2 Beat egg whites in small bowl with electric mixer until soft peaks form. Gradually add sugar, 1 tablespoon at a time, beating until sugar dissolves between additions; fold in cornflour, vinegar and extract.
3 Divide meringue mixture among four shallow ¾-cup (180ml) ovenproof dishes. Place dishes on baking tray; bake, uncovered, in very low oven about 1 hour or until meringues are firm.
4 Meanwhile, melt butter in small saucepan, add cream, extra sugar and spices; bring to a boil. Reduce heat; simmer, uncovered, about 2 minutes or until mixture thickens slightly.
5 Divide banana slices among meringues; drizzle with caramel sauce.

preparation time 15 minutes
cooking time 1 hour
serves 4
per serving 7.5g fat; 1463kJ (350 cal)

caramelised figs with spiced yogurt

1 cup (280g) low-fat plain yogurt
¼ cup (35g) toasted pistachios,
    chopped coarsely
¼ teaspoon ground nutmeg
1 tablespoon caster sugar
6 large fresh figs (480g)
1 tablespoon honey

1 Combine yogurt, nuts, nutmeg and sugar in small bowl.
2 Halve figs lengthways. Brush cut-side of figs with honey.
3 Cook figs, cut-side down, uncovered, in heated large non-stick frying pan 5 minutes. Turn figs; cook, uncovered, 5 minutes or until browned lightly. Serve figs with spiced yogurt.

preparation time 10 minutes
cooking time 10 minutes
serves 4
per serving 6g fat; 777kJ (186 cal)

sticky ginger pears
with cinnamon cream

40g butter
4 medium pears (920g), peeled, halved
  lengthways
⅓ cup (75g) firmly packed brown sugar
1 teaspoon ground cardamom
2 tablespoons green ginger wine
⅔ cup (160ml) double cream
½ teaspoon cinnamon
1 teaspoon icing sugar

1 Heat butter in large heavy-base frying pan; cook pears, sugar, cardamom and ginger wine over high heat, stirring occasionally, about 5 minutes or until pears are browned.
2 Stir the cinnamon and icing sugar into the cream.
3 Serve hot pears with the cream.

preparation time 10 minutes
cooking time 7 minutes
serves 4
per serving 29.3g fat; 1847kJ (441 cal)

glossary

allspice also known as pimento or jamaican pepper; available whole or ground.

aubergine also known as eggplant. Depending on their age, they may have to be sliced and salted to reduce their bitterness. Rinse and dry well before use.

baby also known as japanese eggplant, these are small and slender. They don't need to be salted before use.

bamboo shoots the tender shoots of bamboo plants, available in cans; must be drained and rinsed before use.

barley a nutritious grain used in soups and stews. Hulled barley is the least processed form of barley and is high in fibre. Pearl barley has had the husk discarded and been hulled and polished, much the same as rice.

basil an aromatic herb; there are many types, but the most commonly used is sweet basil.

purple also known as opal basil, has an intense aroma and a longer shelf life than sweet basil.

thai also known as bai kaprow or holy basil; has small crinkly leaves, purple stems and a strong, slightly bitter flavour.

bay leaves aromatic leaves from the bay tree used to flavour soups, stocks and casseroles.

beansprouts also known as bean shoots; tender new growths of assorted beans and seeds germinated for consumption as sprouts.

beans

butterbeans also known as lima beans, sold both dried and canned. A large beige bean having a mealy texture and mild taste.

cannellini small, dried white bean similar to other Phaseolus vulgaris (great northern, navy and haricot beans).

beetroot also known as beets or red beets; firm, round sweet root vegetable.

black bean sauce made from salted and fermented soybeans, spices and wheat flour.

black mustard seeds also known as brown mustard seeds; more pungent than the white (or yellow) seeds used in most prepared mustards.

buttermilk fresh low-fat milk cultured to give a slightly sour, tangy taste; low-fat yogurt or milk can be substituted.

cabanossi a ready-to-eat thin Polish sausage; also known as cabana.

cajun seasoning used to give an authentic USA Deep South spicy cajun flavour to food, this packaged blend of assorted herbs and spices can include paprika, basil, onion, fennel, thyme, cayenne and tarragon.

capers the grey-green buds of a warm climate shrub sold either dried and salted or pickled in vinegar brine.

caraway seeds a member of the parsley family; available in seed or ground form.

caraway seeds a member of the parsley family; available in seed or ground form.

cardamom can be bought in pod, seed or ground form. Has an aromatic, sweetly rich flavour.

cayenne pepper thin-fleshed, long, very-hot red chilli; usually purchased dried and ground.

cheese

cheddar the most common cow's milk 'tasty' cheese; should be aged and hard.

cottage fresh, white, unripened curd cheese with a grainy consistency.

feta a crumbly textured goat's- or sheep's-milk cheese with a sharp, salty taste.

mozzarella a semi-soft cheese with a delicate, fresh taste; has a low melting point and stringy texture when hot.

parmesan a sharp-tasting, dry, hard cheese, made from skimmed or semi-skimmed milk and aged for at least a year.

ricotta a sweet, fairly moist, fresh curd cheese having a low fat content.

chervil also known as cicily; mildly fennel-flavoured herb with curly dark-green leaves.

chickpeas also called garbanzos, hummus or channa; an irregularly round, sandy-coloured legume.

chillies available in many types and sizes, both fresh and dried. The smaller the chilli, the hotter it is. Wear rubber gloves when handling chillies, as they can burn your skin. Removing seeds and membranes lessens the heat level.

chilli powder the Asian variety is the hottest, made from ground chillies; it can be used as a substitute for fresh chillies in the proportion of ½ teaspoon ground chilli powder to 1 medium chopped fresh chilli.

thai small, medium hot, and bright-red to dark-green in colour.

chinese broccoli also known as gai larn. Every part of chinese broccoli is edible.

chinese cabbage also known as peking or napa cabbage, wong bok and petsai, the pale green, crinkly leaves of this elongated cabbage only require brief cooking.

chinese rice wine made from rice wine lees, salt and alcohol; it can be replaced with a pale dry sherry if unavailable.

chives related to the onion and leek, with subtle onion flavour.

chorizo a Spanish sausage made of coarsely ground pork and highly seasoned with garlic and chillies.

choy sum also known as flowering bok choy, flowering white, or chinese flowering, cabbage. The stems, leaves and yellow flowers are served steamed, stir-fried and in soups.

ciabatta meaning 'slipper' in Italian, the traditional shape of this popular crisp-crusted white bread.

cinnamon stick the dried inner bark of the shoots of the cinnamon tree. Also available in ground form.

cloves dried flower buds of a tropical tree; can either be used whole or in ground form.

coconut

cream obtained from the first pressing of the coconut flesh, without the addition of water. Available in cans and cartons.

milk unsweetened coconut milk available in cans.

coriander

dried a fragrant herb; coriander seeds and ground coriander must never be used to replace fresh coriander or vice versa. The tastes are completely different.

fresh also known as cilantro or chinese parsley, bright-green-leafed herb with a pungent flavour.

couscous a fine, grain-like cereal product, made from semolina.

cream we used fresh cream in this book, unless otherwise stated. Also known as pure cream and pouring cream; has no additives unlike commercially thickened cream. Minimum fat content 35%.

soured a thick commercially-cultured soured cream. Minimum fat content 35%.

cumin available both ground and as whole seeds; cumin has a warm, earthy, rather strong flavour.

curry powder a blend of ground spices; choose mild or hot to suit your taste and the recipe.

fish sauce also called nam pla or nuoc nam; made from pulverised salted fermented fish, mostly anchovies. Has a pungent smell and strong taste; use sparingly.

five-spice powder a fragrant mixture of ground cinnamon, cloves, star anise, sichuan pepper and fennel seeds.

flat-leaf parsley also known as continental parsley or italian parsley.

garam masala a blend of spices based on varying proportions of cardamom, cinnamon, cloves, coriander, fennel and cumin, roasted and ground together. Black pepper and chilli can be added for a hotter version.

garlic chives a Chinese herb similar to chives but with a mild garlic flavour.

ghee a pure butter fat available in cans; can be heated to high temperatures without burning due to its lack of salt and milk solids.

ginger also known as green or root ginger; the thick gnarled root of a tropical plant.

pickled available, packaged, from Asian food stores; pickled paper-thin shavings of ginger preserved in a mixture of vinegar, sugar and natural colouring.

green ginger wine beverage 14% alcohol by volume, has the taste of fresh ginger. In cooking, substitute dry (white) vermouth if you prefer.

green split peas also known as field peas; green or yellow pulse grown especially for drying, split in half along a centre seam.

harissa sauce or paste made from dried red chillies, garlic, oil and sometimes caraway seeds.

kaffir lime leaves aromatic leaves used fresh or dried in Asian dishes.

kecap manis an Indonesian sweet, thick soy sauce which has sugar and spices added.

lemongrass a tall, clumping, lemon-smelling and tasting, sharp edged grass; only the white lower part of each stem is used in cooking.

lemon pepper seasoning a blend of black pepper, lemon, herbs and spices.

lemon thyme a variety of thyme with a lemony fragrance.

lentils (red, brown, yellow) dried pulses often identified by and named after their colour.

french green originally from France, these are a small, dark-green, fast-cooking lentils with a delicate flavour.

mangetout ('eat all') also known as snow peas.

mayonnaise we use whole-egg mayonnaise in our recipes.

mirin a champagne-coloured Japanese cooking wine made expressly for cooking and should not be confused with sake.

mixed spice a blend of ground spices usually consisting of cinnamon, allspice and nutmeg.

mushrooms

button small, cultivated white mushrooms having a delicate, subtle flavour.

chestnut light to dark brown mushrooms with full-bodied flavour. Button or cup mushrooms can be substituted for chestnut mushrooms.

oyster lso known as abalone; a grey-white mushroom shaped like a fan. Smooth, with a subtle, oyster-like flavour.

shiitake when fresh are also known as chinese black, forest or golden oak mushrooms; they have an earthy taste. When dried, are known as donko or dried chinese mushrooms; rehydrate before use.

mustard

powder finely ground white (yellow) mustard seeds.

dijon a pale brown, distinctively flavoured fairly mild French mustard.

french plain mild mustard.

wholegrain also known as. seeded A French-style coarse-grain mustard made from crushed mustard seeds and Dijon-style French mustard.

nashi pear also called japanese or asian pear; a member of the pear family, but similar in appearance to an apple.

nutmeg available whole or in ground form.

noodles

dried rice stick made from rice flour and water, available flat and wide or very thin (vermicelli). Soak in boiling water to soften.

hokkien also known as stir-fry noodles; fresh wheat flour noodles resembling thick, yellow-brown spaghetti, needing no pre-cooking before being used.

rice vermicelli also known as rice-flour noodles and rice-stick noodles; made from ground rice. Sold dried, these noodles are best either deep-fried, or soaked then stir-fried or used in soups.

soba Japanese dried noodles made of buckwheat flour.

oil

olive mono-unsaturated; made from the pressing of tree-ripened olives. Extra virgin and virgin are the best, obtained from the first pressings of the olive, while extra light or light refers to the taste, not fat levels.

groundnut pressed from ground peanuts; most commonly used in Asian cooking because of its high smoke point.

sesame made from roasted, crushed, white sesame seeds; a flavouring rather than a cooking medium.

oyster sauce rich sauce made from oysters and their brine, salt, soy sauce and starches.

pak choy also called pak choi or Chinese chard; has a mild mustard taste and is good braised or in stir-fries. Baby pak choy is also available.

palm sugar made from the sap of the sugar palm tree. Light brown to black in colour and usually sold in rock-hard cakes. Substitute brown sugar, if preferred.

paprika ground dried red bell pepper (capsicum); available sweet or hot.

pepper also known as capsicum or bell pepper; seeds and membranes should be discarded before use.

peppercorns available in black, white, red or green.

sichuan peppercorns also known as szechuan or chinese pepper. Small, reddish-brown berries with distinctive peppery-lemon flavour and aroma.

pesto a paste made from fresh basil, oil, garlic, pine nuts and parmesan.

pine nuts also known as pignoli; small, cream-coloured kernels obtained from the cones of different varieties of pine trees.

pistachios pale green, delicately flavoured nut inside hard off-white shells. To peel, soak shelled nuts in boiling water about 5 minutes; drain, then pat dry.

polenta also known as cornmeal; a flour-like cereal made of dried, ground corn (maize).

preserved lemon whole or quartered salted lemons preserved in a mixture of olive oil and lemon juice; imparts a rich, salty-sour acidic flavour. Available from good food shops and delicatessens. Rinse well under cold water before using.

prosciutto salt-cured, air-dried (unsmoked) pressed ham; usually sold in paper-thin slices, ready to eat.

rice

basmati a white fragrant long-grain rice. It should be washed several times before cooking.

jasmine a fragrant long-grained rice; white rice can be substituted but will not taste the same.

long grain elongated grain, remains separate when cooked; most popular steaming rice in Asia.

risoni also known as risi; small rice-shaped pasta very similar to another small pasta, orzo. Any small soup pasta can be substituted for risoni.

rocket also known as arugula, rugula and rucola; a peppery-tasting green leaf. Also baby rocket.

saffron stigma of a member of crocus family, available in strands or ground form; imparts a yellow-orange colour to food. Quality varies – the best is the most expensive spice in the world. Store in freezer.

sake Japanese rice wine. If unavailable, dry sherry, vermouth or brandy may be substituted.

sambal oelek a salty paste made from ground chillies.

sesame seeds black and white are the most common of these tiny oval seeds; a good source of calcium.

shrimp paste a pungent flavoured, strong-scented, firm preserved paste made of salted dried shrimp. Should be chopped or sliced thinly then wrapped in foil and roasted before use.

soy sauce made from fermented soy beans; several variations are available.

star anise a star-shaped pod whose seeds have an astringent aniseed flavour; used to flavour stocks.

sumac a purple-red, astringent spice ground from berries growing on shrubs that flourish wild around the Mediterranean; adds a tart, lemony flavour.

sun-dried tomatoes dried tomatoes sometimes bottled in oil.

sweet chilli sauce mild, Thai sauce made from red chillies, sugar, garlic and vinegar.

tamarind paste made from the pods of a tree native to India that contain a sour-sweet pulp that is dried then reconstituted to make the dark, thick paste that adds a tangy astringent taste to curries. It can also be used in marinades and bastes for meats.

teriyaki sauce a sauce made from soy sauce, corn syrup, vinegar, ginger and other spices; a distinctive glaze on grilled meats.

thai basil also known as horapa, is different from basil and sweet basil in both look and taste. Having smaller leaves and purplish stems, thai basil has a slight liquorice or aniseed taste and is one of the basic flavours that typify Thai cuisine.

tomato

paste triple-concentrated tomato puree used to flavour soups, stews, sauces and casseroles.

plum also known as egg or roma, smallish, oval-shaped tomatoes.

cherry also known as tiny tim or tom thumb tomatoes; small and round.

tortillas unleavened, round bread; available frozen, fresh or vacuum-packed.

turmeric a member of the ginger family, its root is dried and ground; intensely pungent in taste but not hot.

tzatziki greek yogurt and cucumber dish sometimes containing mint and/or garlic.

vanilla extract obtained from vanilla beans infused in water; a non-alcoholic version of essence.

vietnamese mint a pungent and peppery narrow-leafed member of the buckwheat family. A common ingredient in Asian foods, particularly soups, salads and stir-fries.

vine leaves available fresh or vacuum-packed in brine. Available from Middle-Eastern food stores.

vinegar

balsamic authentic only from the province of Modena, Italy; made from a regional wine of white trebbiano grapes specially processed then aged in antique wooden casks to give the exquisite pungent flavour.

cider made from fermented apples.

red wine based on fermented red wine.

rice based on fermented rice.

sherry natural vinegar aged in oak according to the traditional Spanish system.

white made from spirit of cane sugar.

white wine based on fermented white wine.

watercress one of the cress family, a large group of peppery greens used raw in salads, dips and sandwiches, or cooked in soups. Highly perishable, so must be used as soon as possible after purchase.

ACP BOOKS

General manager Christine Whiston
Test kitchen food director Pamela Clark
Editorial director Susan Tomnay
Creative director Hieu Chi Nguyen
Director of sales Brian Cearnes
Marketing manager Bridget Cody
Business analyst Rebecca Varela
Operations manager David Scotto
International rights enquiries Laura Bamford
lbamford@acpuk.com

ACP Books are published by ACP Magazines a division of PBL Media Pty Limited
Publishing Director, Women's Lifestyle
Pat Ingram
Director of sales, Women's lifestyle
Lynette Phillips
Commercial manager, Women's lifestyle
Seymour Cohen
Marketing director, Women's lifestyle
Matthew Dominello
Public relations manager, Women's lifestyle
Hannah Deveraux
Creative director, Events, Women's lifestyle
Luke Bonnano
Research Director, Women's lifestyle
Justin Stone
PBL Media, Chief Executive officer
Ian Law

Produced by ACP Books, Sydney.
Published by ACP Books, a division of ACP Magazines Ltd, 54 Park St, Sydney; GPO Box 4088, Sydney, NSW 2001.
phone (02) 9282 8618 fax (02) 9267 9438.
acpbooks@acpmagazines.com.au
www.acpbooks.com.au
Printed and bound in China.

Australia Distributed by Network Services, phone +61 2 9282 8777 fax +61 2 9264 3278
networkweb@networkservicescompany.com.au
United Kingdom Distributed by Australian Consolidated Press (UK),
phone (01604) 642 200 fax (01604) 642 300
books@acpuk.com
New Zealand Distributed by Netlink Distribution Company,
phone (9) 366 9966 ask@ndc.co.nz
South Africa Distributed by PSD Promotions, phone (27 11) 392 6065/6/7
fax (27 11) 392 6079/80
orders@psdprom.co.za
Canada Distributed by Publishers Group Canada phone (800) 663 5714 fax (800) 565 3770
service@raincoast.com

A catalogue record for this book is available from the British Library.
ISBN 978-1-903777-53-4
© ACP Magazines Ltd 2008
ABN 18 053 273 546